HANDY DAD

HANDY DAD

BY TODD DAVIS

PHOTOGRAPHS BY JULI STEWART AND TODD DAVIS
ILLUSTRATIONS BY NIK SCHULZ

25 AWESOME PROJECTS
FOR DADS AND KIDS

CHRONICLE BOOKS
SAN FRANCISCO

Text copyright © 2010 by Todd Davis.
Photographs copyright © 2010 by Juli Stewart and Todd Davis.
Illustrations copyright © 2010 by Nik Schulz.

Library of Congress Cataloging-in-Publication Data:

Davis, Todd, 1972–
    Handy Dad : 25 awesome projects for dad and kids / Todd Davis
        p. cm.
    ISBN: 978-0-8118-6958-4
    1. Handicraft—Design. 2. Toy making. 3. Family recreation.
  I. Title.

TT157.D382 2010
745.592—dc22

                                                          2009026020

Manufactured in China
Designed by Andrew Schapiro

Production assistance provided by
DC Typography, San Francisco

As with any project, it is important that all instructions are followed
carefully; failure to do so could result in injury. Every effort has been
made to present the information in this book in a clear, complete, and
accurate manner; however, not every situation can be anticipated
and there is no substitute for your own common sense. Check product
labels to make sure that the materials you use are safe and nontoxic.
"Nontoxic" is a description given to any substance that does not give
off dangerous fumes or contain harmful ingredients (such as chemicals
or poisons) in amounts that could endanger a person's health. Be careful when handling dangerous objects. The authors and Chronicle Books
disclaim any and all liability resulting from injuries or damage caused
during the production or use of the crafts discussed in this book.

10 9 8 7 6 5 4 3 2 1

Chronicle Books LLC
680 Second Street
San Francisco, California 94107
www.chroniclebooks.com

This book is dedicated to my dad and my son.

TABLE OF CONTENTS

INTRODUCTION

When I was a kid, I had overwhelming urges to break things, real things: kitchenware, furniture, ceramic re-creations of Sweden, and virtually anything belonging to my sister.

My parents, however, were not willing to encourage this hobby of mine by providing me with any of their own possessions. Determined to teach me the value of material things beyond that of tinder, my father had the clever idea of getting me to build my own toys. In having me go through the process of designing and building airplanes and go-carts and child-sized medieval catapults, I suppose he thought I might come to respect property (other people's and my own), thereby mitigating my sister's trauma in finding bald, one-legged Barbie dolls treading water in the toilet. He was right, at least partially.

I continued to destroy things, even those things my father and I made together, but I did so a bit more gradually. Since I hate having to repair anything, I began to build toys that would last. At the time, I did not grasp that my father was doing more than teaching me how to swing a hammer gracefully while inflicting the fewest number of injuries. In providing me with the space to create, he was teaching me how to see the world differently, how to plan for it, how to make beautiful and occasionally identifiable sketches, and, most important, how to use my imagination toward something that would keep me entertained long enough for my father to take naps.

Over time, my projects with my father took a more sophisticated turn. We built a birdcage to house the pigeons my friends and I caught while exploring a large creek next to the highway; it had a spring-loaded door. Another was a half-pipe with sheet metal spot-welded to the frame. My father continued to give me important advice on my projects even when I was confident enough to build things on my own. I didn't mind—I enjoyed having him around correcting my technique, reminding me not to use his new drill, and calling out the distance between my hand and the serrated teeth of the chop saw.

Designing and building have been invaluable in my life. My childhood experiences led me to pursue a degree in landscape architecture, a career I decided to put on hold after graduation in order to compete in extreme snowboard and skiing competitions. In the years after college, I lived in a snow cave (my own design) in Argentina for one month; broke some records in extreme sports such as skydiving, skiing, snowboarding, mountain biking (downhill), surfing, waterskiing, high diving, and skateboarding; and threw myself off cliffs and buildings for money in movies and commercials. I was the runner-up in HGTV's *Design Star* competition and began hosting a show about home improvements called *Over Your Head*, also on HGTV. I currently run a successful design company called Epic Spaces. The company's principal focus is on creating dynamic, interactive spaces for both outdoor and indoor environments.

When I build, I do so in direct response to other people's work, with the intent of improving upon it. I also always build things for my own use first, which means they must be able to withstand frequent and prolonged physical abuse. Though I sometimes build feverishly, I have come to temper my sense of urgency to bring a project to completion. Making a toy by hand is a lesson in problem solving, and I have learned to cherish those moments with family and friends when we can look critically at a project and make slight changes for the purpose of improving it. Sometimes the suggestions of one's family and friends are not very helpful—like, "Why don't you call your go-cart *Superfast Stuff*?"—but often they can open the proverbial doors of perception and actually teach you something about being a "handy dad."

The projects in this book also have been designed for both indoor and outdoor activities and for both dads and kids to make and enjoy. It is enough to choose an activity that your child is relatively passionate about and then begin experimenting and building together. I do not expect every child who makes a dollhouse from this book to become the next Frank Gehry, but I am confident these projects will stimulate children's creativity and encourage their pursuit of bliss, as well as give fathers something to do with their kids that does not involve computer games or listening to Raffi.

These projects are inspired by the things I liked to do as a kid, things my dad taught me about building, and the risk-taking and extreme sports I've done as an adult. You'll find step-by-step instructions for making a whole range of stuff. Whip up a sweet half-pipe or BMX ramp for the little adventurers in your life; take some time building a tree house, zip line, climbing wall, or tire swing in the backyard to keep your kids and their friends entertained for years on end; spend some quality time indoors building angel wings or a dollhouse that will bring a smile to any little girl's face; throw together a pressurized water rocket, water-balloon launcher, slip-and-slide, or tie-dye station for an afternoon of guaranteed fun. Trust me, the process of building these things with your kids is almost as fun as watching the delight on their faces when they see the finished product.

Fittingly, my wife and I just had a baby boy. He is already beginning to understand how stacking colored blocks into sophisticated little piles can improve his world. Having been taught so many wonderful things by my own father, I cannot wait to encourage my son's growth. I am looking forward to the moment when things go wrong, so I can spend that much more time with him, watching him as he tries to figure out how to make side lashings for his first rope bridge out of lint and dental floss. I know that soon enough he will be fixing the carburetor on his father's car, leaving me behind with my own "handy dad" as we struggle to fix his recliner.

EASY
PROJECTS

LAVA LAMP

When you reminisce about the days of bell-bottoms, Bee Gees, and moonlight skates at the roller rink, do your kids just stare at you blankly? Well, the '70s might not mean much to them, but I bet they'll freak out when they see this mind-blowing icon of awesomeness. All you need to make a totally trippy lava lamp is some oil, water, food coloring, and a little Alka-Seltzer. Plop, plop, fizz, fizz, oh how far-out it is!

DIFFICULTY LEVEL:
Super-easy

TIME INVOLVED:
30 minutes

MATERIALS:

One 4-foot 1×6 redwood board
(you can substitute cedar or pine)

IKEA Dinge lamp (cost: about $3) plus 25-watt light bulb

20 ounces vegetable oil

6 ounces water

Food coloring

26-ounce pasta-sauce jar

Alka-Seltzer tablet

FASTENERS:

1¼-inch wood screws (14)

TOOLS:

Drill with Phillips-head bit, ⅛-inch bit, and 2¼-inch hole-saw attachment

Jigsaw with a multipurpose blade

Circular saw or chop saw

Ruler

Pencil

Two mini bar-clamps

1 From the 1×6 board, cut two pieces that each measure 4¼ × 5 inches. These will be the **A SIDEWALLS**. Label them, if it will help you keep track. Remember that your saw blade will use up ⅛ inch of material as it cuts. Measure carefully.

2 Cut two more pieces that each measure 2¾ × 5 inches. These will be the **B SIDEWALLS**.

3 Cut a small notch out of a corner of one of the **B SIDEWALLS** to accommodate the lamp's power cord.

4 Cut two more pieces of wood that each measure 4 × 4¼ inches. These will form the **TOP** and **BOTTOM** of the base.

5 Take the piece that will be the top and mark its center by placing a ruler diagonally across two opposite corners and drawing a line along its repeat using the other two opposite corners. The point where the lines intersect is the center of the piece. Using your 2¼-inch hole saw, cut a hole in the center. I'd recommend clamping the piece down to a larger piece of scrap wood with some mini bar-clamps to give you some leverage and to ensure a clean cut. See **Finding Center**.

6 Predrill screw holes with a ⅛-inch bit, then attach the **A SIDEWALLS** to the **BOTTOM** piece using two wood screws per sidewall. See image **a**.

7 Place the lamp inside the base and then attach the **B SIDEWALLS** in the same way. Make sure the lamp cord passes through the notch you cut for it before attaching. See image **b**.

8 Predrill screw holes with a ⅛-inch bit, then attach the **A SIDEWALLS** to the **B SIDEWALLS** by driving a wood screw into each of the top corners of the lamp base. See image **c**.

9 Adjust the light to make sure it fits snugly into the base. Predrill screw holes and attach the top piece using wood screws in two opposite corners. See image **d**.

10 To make the "lava juice," combine the vegetable oil with the water and 10 drops of food coloring in the jar. Shake it up (with the lid on), or break an Alka-Seltzer tablet into four pieces and drop in one piece at a time until you get the right amount of fizz. If you use this method, leave room in the top of the jar so the bubbling lava juice doesn't overflow when you add the Alka-Seltzer pieces. Leave the lid off, too—if you pressurize a glass jar it may burst. Put the jar on the base, right-side up, turn on the light, and put on some funky music and chill out.

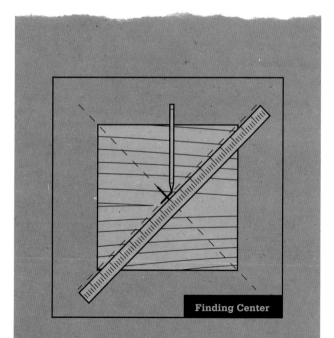

Finding Center

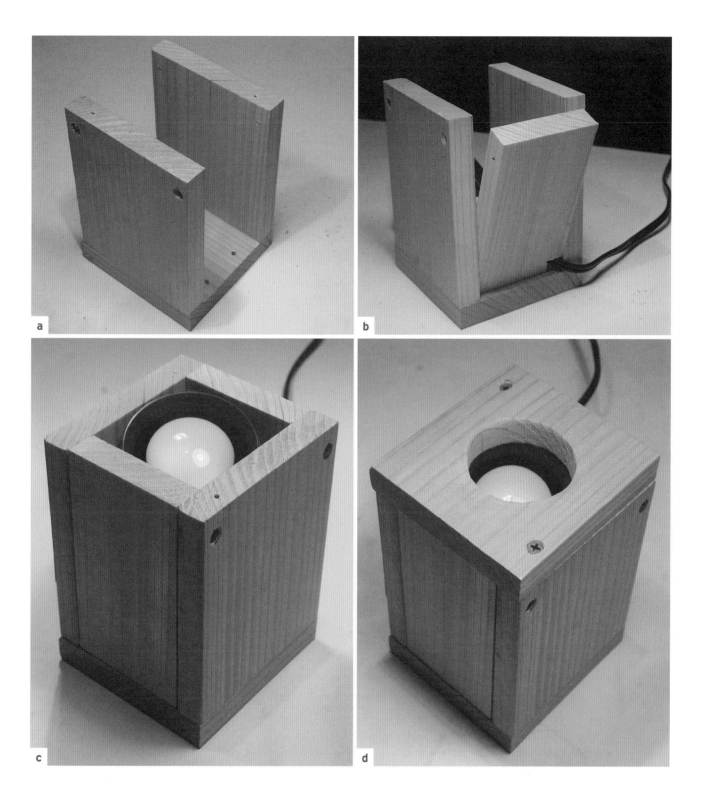

PAPER AIRPLANE: THE BOMBPROOF BOMBER

Remember the classic, pointy paper airplane? Well, I've designed an upgrade. Allow me to introduce the Bombproof Bomber. It's been designed to withstand the most rigorous missions and can be deployed flight after flight in the toughest conditions. It can be launched quickly from any desktop base, or carried stealthily in a back pocket. Not only is it tough, it's also customizable. It can be modified for cruising, high-speed attack, and high- or low-power launches. Not only that, the nose is reinforced to withstand high-velocity impact, yet the plane is balanced enough to ensure smooth, steady flight. It also provides excellent grip for all finger-based launching systems. What's more, planes can be decorated with your own ornamentations, although I prefer a plain white fleet. Here's how you and your kids can manufacture a fleet of your own.

DIFFICULTY LEVEL:
Easy

TIME INVOLVED:
10 minutes

MATERIALS:

8½-×-11-inch sheet of plain paper

TOOLS:

Ruler

1 Fold the sheet of paper in half lengthwise by lining up the corners, holding down the outside edges, and dragging your thumb across the paper to make a fold. (Remember, manufacturing tolerances can make or break a plane. To ensure successful flights, keep the quality control high.) Open the paper.

2 From the top short side of the sheet, fold both corners into the inner seam so that the edges touch. This side of your plane should now look like the point of an arrow. See image **a**.

3 Fold the entire arrow section back onto the plane by lining up the point of the arrow exactly with the inner seam about two-thirds of the way down. The paper should now look like a square. See image **b**.

4 Now take one of the corners formed by your folded arrow and line it up on the center seam of the plane so the edges on either side of the corner form a 45° angle with the center seam. See image **c**. Do the same with the other corner. Here's where you can do some Skunk Works–quality customization, if you want. For example, instead of bringing the corner of the wing flaps all the way to the centerline, keep the 45° angles, but place each corner ⅜ inch away from the center seam. This will give the wings more surface area, which translates to longer flight times. The tradeoff is slower launches.

5 This next step involves a little paper plane craftsman-ship. Remember the arrowhead point that you folded down onto the center seam? Fold it back towards the front of the plane so that it makes a ½-inch tear in the inside edge of the wing flaps. See image **d**.

6 Now fold the entire plane in half along the center seam, so that all of the folded parts are facing out.

7 Take the outside edge of the wing flap and fold it perfectly against the bottom edge of the plane. This tucks all the folds under the wing for smooth flight. Repeat on the other side. See image **e**.

8 Your Bombproof Bomber is complete! Take a minute to do some preflight quality control by pressing the plane flat on its side and smoothing out any kinks in the folds.

9 Alright! It's time for some test flights. Grab the plane between your thumb and index finger at the thickest part of the folds. Push the wings so they're even with one another, and launch that bird into the sky! For maximum range, throw it as hard as you can, launching it at an upward angle of 45°.

10 To add another level of flight-path control, tear ½ inch into the tail of each wing just off the center of the plane and fold up the edges to make a pair of flaps. If you push the flaps up, the plane will climb after take-off. Push them down and it will dive. One up and one down will induce a roll. For straighter flight, add a paper-clip nose cone.

Make a whole squadron, and your kids can have a dogfight! Happy flying!

WATER-PRESSURIZED ROCKET

It's pretty amazing to watch NASA rocket launches from Cape Canaveral. It's even more amazing to watch rocket launches when NASA is in your own backyard. And you won't need a billion-dollar budget. With just a few materials repurposed from around the house—a plastic soda bottle, a cork, and a bike pump—you and your kids will be launching flights high into the atmosphere in no time. Roger that.

DIFFICULTY LEVEL:
Easy

TIME INVOLVED:
A couple of hours

MATERIALS:

Wine bottle cork

Plastic 2-liter soda bottle

Bike pump with ball needle and long hose (2 to 3 feet)

Water to use as "rocket fuel"

TOOLS:

Utility knife

LAUNCH PAD (OPTIONAL)

MATERIALS:

One 6-foot 1×8 redwood or pine fence board

FASTENERS:

2-inch wood screws (10)

TOOLS:

Circular saw or chop saw

Handsaw

Drill with ⅛-inch bit

INSTRUCTIONS:

1 Make sure the cork fits the opening of the soda bottle. If you're having trouble finding a cork that fits, check with your local hardware store. They should be able to help you out.

2 Measure the cork against the needle and use a utility knife to cut off enough of it so the needle just sticks out of the end of the cork when you push it through. See **Cutting the Cork** and image **a**.

3 Now push the needle lengthwise through the center of the cork. See image **b**.

4 Attach the needle to the end of the bike pump hose.

5 Fill the soda bottle one-third full of rocket fuel— I mean, water.

6 Here is where we seal this baby up. Push the cork into the bottle as hard as you can. See image **c**.

7 Make some sort of launch stand that allows you to prop the bottle upside down. A huge cardboard or PVC tube will work well. Even propping it up against a couple of bricks will work. Just make sure the bottle isn't aimed at the middle of someone's forehead. (If you want to make something more official, see the instructions for building a launch pad on page 24.) See image **d**.

8 Have a flight technician (or a kid) start pumping, and count the pumps as the launch sequence progresses. The bottle should fill with bubbles, and the cork will hiss a bit. After 20 or so pumps, you'll reach ignition. (Once you've learned exactly how many pumps it takes, the next time you can start the countdown with that number.) The cork will explode out of the neck and the rocket will blast skyward. Keep an eye on it!

9 Now it's time to send out the recovery team. If you built the rocket right, it will be far away from the launch base. If you had a successful flight, head back to mission control, break out the bubblegum cigars for your crew, and "refuel" for your next flight. If not, head back to the drawing board!

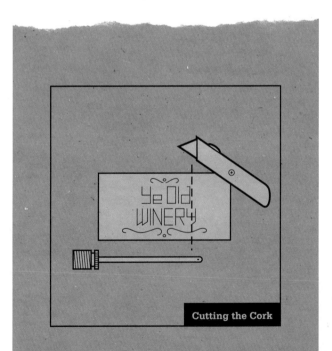

Cutting the Cork

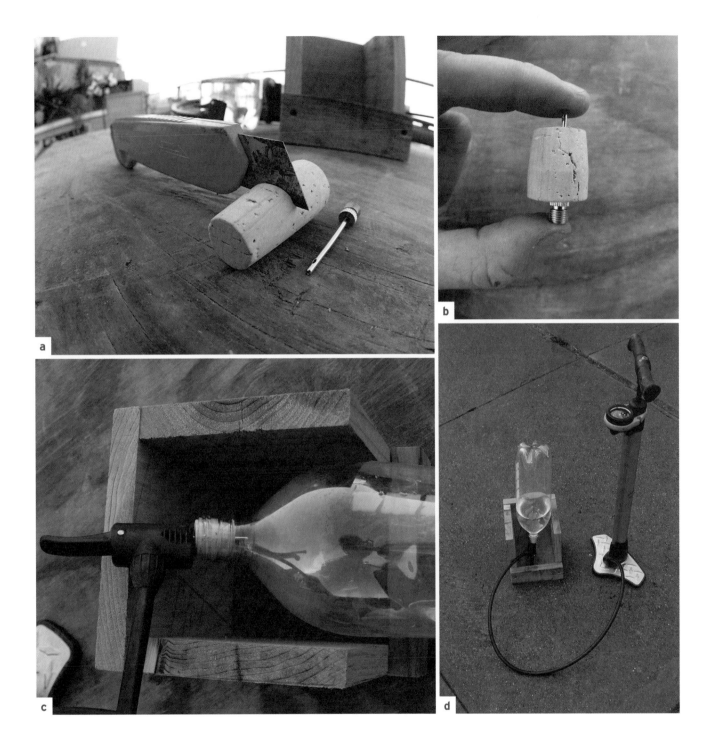

BUILDING A LAUNCH PAD

For optimal flights, build a launch pad to make rocket launches easier.

1 Using your circular saw or chop saw, cut your fence board into two 6½-×-6½-inch pieces.

2 Now cut two more pieces that measure 5½ × 6½ inches. These will be the **SIDEWALLS**.

3 Cut another piece that measures 6½ × 2 inches. This will be the **FRONT LIP** of the base.

4 Predrill all screw holes in this project with a ⅛-inch bit. With two wood screws, attach the two large pieces together at one edge so that they form an L shape. This is the beginning of the base. See image **a**.

5 Attach the **SIDEWALLS** to the L-shaped base to form a three-sided box, driving two wood screws per side through the bottom of the base. All the edges should be flush with one another. See image **b**.

6 Connect the sidewalls to the rear wall by driving one wood screw through the back of the box on each side, about 1 inch down from the top edge.

7 Using two wood screws, attach the **LIP** to the front of the box. Again, make sure all the edges are flush. See image **c**.

You now have a stable base from which to launch the rockets. You can try to aim them, but they'll pretty much go where they want. Start collecting soda bottles now to build up your fleet of H_2O bombs!

Happy flying!

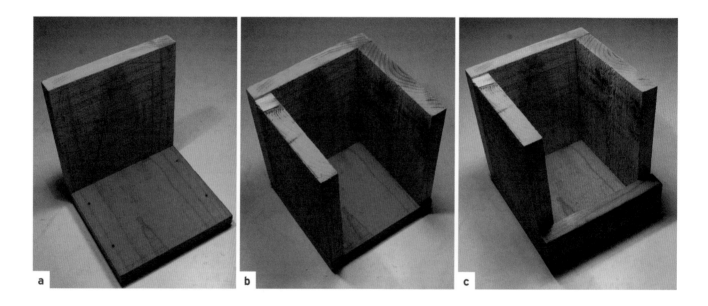

a b c

SLIP-AND-SLIDE

This project is E-Z. It will set up in five minutes, and then your kids can slide themselves silly all day. It just takes a patch of lawn, a little bit of soap, and a few splashes of good ol' H_2O. Boom! Instant water park.

To take this project from easy to epic, add a sandy slope, one of the ramps from the Half-Pipe project (page 126), and your favorite lake. Double-boom! Now you're talkin' launch control!

DIFFICULTY LEVEL:
Easy

TIME INVOLVED:
One beer

MATERIALS:

One 4-×-100-foot roll heavy-duty plastic drop cloth

One bottle biodegradable liquid dish soap

FASTENERS:

Garden U stakes (24; you'll need two to start and an additional two for every 10 feet of slide)

TOOLS:

One bucket of water

1 Find a long, flat patch of lawn that's free of roots, sprinklers, and any other obstacles you wouldn't want your kids to run into in the middle of a full-speed slide. Inclines work too—they're actually better because the kids won't have to "Pete Rose" it as much to get a good ride. Just make sure they'll have a soft landing zone!

2 Unroll a few feet of the tarp and stake down both corners with the U stakes. You should be able to just push them into the lawn by hand. Now unroll the rest of the tarp, adding a pair of stakes (one per side) every 10 feet and another pair at the end of the slide.

3 Apply a little soap along the length of the tarp. One soaping will last four or five slides.

4 Wet the tarp with a little water before each slide. You won't need much.

5 That's it! Now have one of your slide testers get a huge running start and launch into a slide right at the beginning of the tarp. Don't worry—if they forget to go into slide mode, the slip-and-slide will take care of this automatically!

When your team of sliders is done for the day, rinse off the slip-and-slide and let it dry before putting it away; otherwise it will turn into a mold-and-mildew mess.

How was that? Did your kids have a good time? Great! A day at the water park, and you didn't even have to buy tickets! Pretty cool.

AFTERNOON PROJECTS

TIE-DYE

What do you do when your kids keep asking for clothes that look like they were made with pictures from the Hubble Space Telescope? Or what if they want to look like they're bending the very fabric of space and time? Or what if they simply spend a lot of time at psychedelic chameleon conventions and want to blend in? The trouble with any normal clothes you may find is that they're of absolutely no help in any of these situations. Whether you face these types of dilemmas on a daily basis or just want to clothe your off-spring in a mind-blowing wonderland of color, tie-dye is the answer.

DIFFICULTY LEVEL:
Pretty Easy

TIME INVOLVED:
An afternoon

MATERIALS:

Anything cotton that you'd like to add color to—shirts, pillowcases, sheets, pants, etc. (Hemp, rayon, and linen will also work, but 100 percent cotton is best.)

Plastic grocery bags or kitchen trash bags

THE FOLLOWING CAN BE FOUND AT YOUR LOCAL ARTS AND CRAFTS STORE:

Soda ash, to help fabric absorb the dye better (Soda ash is sold in 1-pound bags. Our recipe calls for a cup, but you may need to add a bit more, depending on how much fabric you are dyeing.)

Procion MX fiber-reactive dye (Start with a 3-ounce jar each of red, blue, and yellow, with a jar of black for contrast. *Don't use Rit dye; it doesn't work well for tie-dyeing.*)

FASTENERS:

Rubber bands, in various sizes (50)

TOOLS:

5-gallon bucket

Rubber gloves (get good ones)

8-ounce plastic squeeze bottles with removable pointed tips (one for each color you're using)

Teaspoon

Measuring cup

Cooking grill or wire mesh

Plastic tray that the grill/mesh will fit over

Plastic bags (as many as what you are dyeing)

Stove

Plastic spatula

Rags

Washable felt-tip pen

1 Collect all the clothes and fabric you want to awesome-ize.

2 Grab the bucket and add a cup of soda ash and 1 gallon of very warm water, heated on the stove. Stir with the plastic spatula until dissolved. (This is enough for about 10 shirts; simply add more for more fabric.)

3 Soak the fabric in this mixture for 15 minutes.

4 With your rubber gloves on, pull out the first piece you'd like to dye and wring it out over the bucket. See image **a**.

5 Let's start with an easy twist pattern, and let's say we're doing shirts. After you've wrung the first one out, shake it loose, then grab both ends and twist them in opposite directions. Once it's wound up tight, secure it with plenty of rubber bands and set it aside.

6 Grab another shirt, wring it out, and lay it flat on a table (make sure the table is clean and free of any debris or dye), front-side down.

7 Let's try a sunburst pattern now. Pick a spot to be the center of the sunburst and pinch the fabric between your fingers. See image **b**. Be sure to pinch both the top and bottom layers of the shirt. Now spin with your fingers in place until you've twisted the shirt into a tight spiral. See image **c**. Keep spinning it and cup your free hand around the outside of the bundle to collect any stray sleeves or corners into a nice, tight, patty-like disc.

8 Stretch out a rubber band and carefully slide the bottom edge of it under the fabric disc you've made. Add two or three more rubber bands to hold all the edges of the fabric. Make sure all the rubber bands cross each other in the center of the disc. See image **d**. If you turn the disc over, you'll notice that the spiral is better on the side that was against the table. A tighter spiral will

produce a better result. That's why we put the front side facing down. Put the shirt aside for later.

9 A V-pattern is more advanced. For this one, lay the shirt flat on the table as before, but fold it down the middle, lengthwise. Now, using a washable felt-tip pen, draw a curved line from the shoulder of the shirt to the folded edge, about 3 inches from the bottom. Starting at the bottom, fold the shirt up in 1-inch folds. (See image **e**.) The folds should be perpendicular to the line you drew and follow it all the way up to the shoulder. Be sure to press flat on every one. See image **f**. Secure with plenty of rubber bands—you can use smaller ones here.

10 Okay, let's mix up the dye. In each squeeze bottle, combine 2 teaspoons of a single color with 8 ounces of water. Mix as many bottles as you like. Are the lids on tight? (You want to make sure to dye the clothes on the table, not the ones you have on.) Good. Now shake well.

11 Place the grill over your plastic container. I took the grill out of my oven and placed it over the kitchen sink, which worked fine. Just remember to rinse it off right after you're done. Tie-dye is cool. Tie-dyed pork roast, not so much.

12 Alright, Jackson Pollock, this is where the fun begins. Let's grab that first twisted shirt and put it in the middle of the rack. What colors do you want to use? Grab two for starters. Now this takes a bit of finesse. You'll want to add enough color to make the white of the shirt disappear, but not so much to totally soak it through. The idea is to end up with more dye on the areas of the shirt that are exposed and less in the folds. See images **g** and **h**, page 35. This differentiation is what gives the shirt its magic. It might take a couple of tries to find the sweet spot in terms of dye application. You also might notice that colors blend together to form new colors. So even though you've started with only three colors, you can make any color

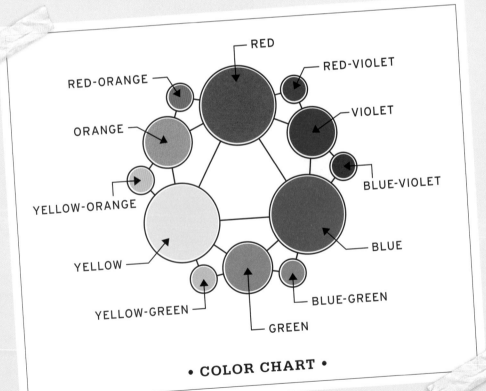

RED

RED-VIOLET

RED-ORANGE

VIOLET

ORANGE

BLUE-VIOLET

YELLOW-ORANGE

YELLOW

BLUE

YELLOW-GREEN

BLUE-GREEN

GREEN

• COLOR CHART •

by blending them in varying amounts on the shirt. We've provided a color chart to help you along.

13 Is your masterwork finished? If so, then place it in a plastic bag, seal it up, and store it in a warm room for 24 hours. Grab your next shirt. Try adding a third color this time. When you're done, seal each shirt as described above. Don't forget to rinse the sink and the grill rack when you're done!

14 Okay, through the magic of book writing, it's 24 hours later. Take the shirts out of the bags and remove the rubber bands. How awesome do they look? Pretty awesome, right? Great. Rinse the shirts out with cold water until no more dye comes out when you squeeze them.

15 Now hang them to dry on a hanger in the shower or on a clothesline. DO NOT THROW THEM IN THE DRYER. If you machine-dry them while the dye is still wet, the colors will bleed and it will look like mush.

16 That's it. Your kids are now ready to start their own magical mystery tour! When the tour's over and you need to wash their shirts for the first time, do so in cold water just to make sure the colors don't bleed all over your non-far-out clothes. (You can machine dry them now.)

17 If all your kids' friends make shirts, too, they can sit across from each other in a circle and totally trip on all of the colors! So awesome! Don't forget to provide drums to heighten the effect.

g

h

ROPE SWING

Backyard rope swings, about as American as baseball, apple pie, and Tarzan, will entertain for years to come. You just can't beat the fun-to-dollar ratio of a hank of rope, a scrap of wood, and an old faithful tree.* A couple of knots are all you need.

* *The swingin' branch should be at least 6 inches thick and over 8 feet above the ground.*

MATERIALS:

¾-inch or thicker twisted nylon rope*
(length depends on height of branch)

Garden hose (3-foot section)

8-inch 2×6 redwood board

* *A quick note about nylon rope: It's one of the strongest general-purpose ropes you can get. It will last four to five times longer than a natural-fiber rope because of its higher abrasion resistance and good resistance to chemicals, oil, and UV light (sunshine). Twisted nylon rope, as opposed to braided rope, also has the ability to stretch and snap back into shape. This makes it great for absorbing shock loads, like the kind generated when 80-pound kids reach the bottom of their swinging arcs.*

TOOLS:

Drill with ¾-inch spade or auger bit

Sandpaper, 60-grit

Cigarette or grill lighter

NOTE: For details on tying the knots referred to in this project, refer to the Knots section on page 162.

INSTRUCTIONS:

1 Locate a tree and requisite branch. Bigger and higher is always better. If you find a 6-inch branch 90 feet up, call me. I want to swing from that baby!

2 You'll want to have enough rope to make it from the ground to the branch with about 6 feet left over. Just get more rope than you think you'll need. It's got a million uses, and it's better to have too much than too little. Grab what will be the tree-branch end of the rope and heat it with the lighter to prevent it from fraying. When, in a minute or so, you see that all of the fibers have melted together, it's done.

3 This would be a good time to practice tying a bow-line. Since you'll be using a garden hose, there's no need to take an extra turn around the object as described in the instructions.

4 Okay, let's do this thing. Tie a stopper knot 8 feet from the tree-branch end of the rope. Slide the garden hose over the tied-off end of the rope, stick the tail end in your back pocket, and climb the tree. I always take the adventurous route, but you can use a ladder too, if the branch is close enough.

5 Read ahead a bit now—don't go taking this book into the tree with you! Reading these instructions while you're hanging from a 50-foot-long branch is like calling the IRS and telling them you skipped a few steps on your taxes. It's just asking for trouble.

6 Okay, you'll be bear-hugging the branch with your legs. Don't look down. Place the hose-covered section of rope on the branch about 8 feet from the trunk. Make sure to leave about 2 feet of rope sticking out past the end of the hose.

7 Next comes the moment of truth. Tie the bowline. Leave enough slack in it so you can put a fist through the loop. This will allow for some movement while preventing excessive rubbing among the rope, hose, and tree.

8 Check to make sure the knot is tight. If it is, you're golden and can monkey your way down from the tree.

9 Now grab the piece of redwood. This will be the swing step. Drill a ¾-inch hole through the center of it and give all the edges a good sanding.

10 Tie three stopper knots in the rope—6 feet, 5 feet, and 4 feet off the ground.

11 Pull the rope through the hole in the swing step, positioning it 3 feet off of the ground. Tie two stopper knots in the rope directly beneath the step.

12 Now you should have a perfect swinging platform. Cut off the rest of the rope a few inches above the ground and melt the end with the lighter as before.

As I said, any leftover rope will have a million uses—a jump rope for instance. Hey, two projects in one!

LION-MANE TIRE SWING

The oldest piece of junk can be the coolest thing in the world. Take old tires, for instance. Some people see them as an eyesore. But what do you see? That's right . . . many kid-hours of fun. Old tires make excellent tire swings. What you'll need for this project is a big tree with a thick horizontal branch (almost as thick as the trunk) that's about 10 feet or more off the ground and relatively horizontal. You don't have any old tires in your backyard? No worries. Head down to the nearest auto repair shop with your children in tow. They'll have plenty of tires for you to choose from. Look for a low-profile tire (that means the hole in the middle is bigger and the tire itself is wider), which makes for better swinging. Just ask your kids to hang on to the lion's mane (the rope handles) while they're going koo-koo-ape bonkers.

DIFFICULTY LEVEL:
Easy

TIME INVOLVED:
An afternoon

MATERIALS:

High-performance, low-profile tire

40 feet heavy-duty ¾-inch nylon rope

3 feet ⅜-inch-thick chain

3 feet clear plastic 2-inch tubing

FASTENERS:

2-inch eyebolt with two nuts (1)

¼-inch galvanized washers (2)

½-inch galvanized washers (2)

⅜-inch quick link (1)

Double-eye swivel (1)

TOOLS:

Drill with ¼-inch bit and 1-inch auger bit

Wire-cutting pliers

Cigarette or grill lighter

Duct tape

Ladder long enough to reach your chosen branch

NOTE: For details on tying the knots referred to in this project, refer to the Knots section on page 162.

1 Drill a ¼-inch hole in the middle of the top and bottom of the tire. The top hole is for the eyebolt. The bottom hole is so you don't create your own mosquito hatchery: no water in the bottom of the tire means no mosquitoes (from your tire swing, anyway).

2 Slide a ¼-inch washer, then a ½-inch washer, onto the 2-inch eyebolt and insert it into one of the holes. This will be the top of the swing. See image **a**.

3 Turn the tire upside down. Find the end of the eyebolt and put a ½-inch washer, then a ¼-inch washer on the end of it. Screw on a nut and tighten it all the way down. Now add the other nut and tighten that one down on the first one, locking them together forever.

4 Turn the tire right-side up. With a 1-inch drill bit, drill four holes 1 inch or so from the edge of the tire and 10 inches from the eyebolt, forming a rectangle. See **Drilling Holes in the Tire**. This will allow someone to sit on top of the tire without the rope holds getting in their way.

5 If you see any frayed or stray wires sticking out from the body of the tire, clip them off with the pliers. Make sure there aren't any sharp edges left over.

6 From the rope, cut four 2-foot pieces. Heat the ends with the lighter and wrap them with duct tape to keep them from fraying.

7 Tie a stopper knot in one end of each piece of rope and insert the unknotted ends into the 1-inch holes. Once they're through the holes, tie stopper knots in the other ends. See image **b**.

8 Put the chain inside the plastic tubing. This will protect the tree from being chafed by the chain.

9 Place your ladder (make sure the feet are on solid, level ground), climb up with your chain, lay it over your chosen branch, and connect the two ends with the ⅜-inch quick link. Before you close it, insert one end of the double-eye swivel. Okay, now tighten up the quick link. See image **c**.

10 Did you heat and tape off the end of the rope already? Good. Then tie it to the other end of the double-eye swivel with a bowline, taking an extra turn through the eye of the swivel when you make the loop.

11 Pass the other end of the rope through the eyebolt on the tire, adjust the height to your preference, and tie it off with another bowline, taking an extra loop through the eyebolt. Trim any excess rope.

12 Watch your kids pile on and swing themselves silly!

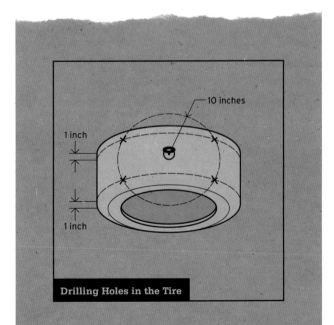

1 inch
10 inches
1 inch
1 inch

Drilling Holes in the Tire

SLINGSHOT

A trusty slingshot can come in handy on any number of occasions. Does your son need to be able to snap a piece of bark at his girlfriend's window to signal a secret rendezvous? Does your daughter need to be able to drop tin cans from a fence? Do either of them have an urge to do some high-powered rock-skipping down at the pond? Don't tell your kids this, but I used to zing pebbles at my brother's back, then yell, "Ahhh! Beeeeees!" while running away, pretending I too had just been "stung." Heh heh. Whether this gets your kids into trouble or keeps them out of it is their call, but slingshots are always fun to have around.

DIFFICULTY LEVEL:
Challenging

TIME INVOLVED:
An afternoon

MATERIALS:

One freshly cut, Y-shaped stick (An ideal stick will have a handle that's ½ inch to 1 inch thick and 7 inches long, and arms ½ inch to ¾ inch thick, 4 inches to 7 inches long, and 4 inches to 7 inches apart.)

2 feet ⁷⁄₁₆-inch surgical tubing with ¼-inch core diameter (Available at scuba gear retailers such as reefscuba.com.)

12 inches ¼-inch poly tubing

One work glove with suede leather palm

FASTENERS:

16 feet ¹⁄₁₆-inch twisted nylon twine

Athletic tape (1 roll)

Gorilla Glue

TOOLS:

Sandpaper, 60-grit

Pocketknife

INSTRUCTIONS:

1 Remove any burls or bumps to make all the limbs of the Y-stick smooth. Also sand down and round off the cut edges a bit.

2 Cut the surgical tubing into two 12-inch-long pieces.

3 From the poly tubing, cut two 3-inch pieces.

4 Slide a 3-inch piece of poly tubing into one end of each piece of surgical tubing. Push it in until the ends are flush.

5 Cut a 2-×-4-inch piece of suede out of the palm of the work glove. Round off both the long sides so you end up with a piece that looks like a blunt football. It should still be 4 inches long and 2 inches wide in the middle, but only 1 inch wide on the ends.

6 Now make a $\frac{7}{16}$-inch cut $\frac{1}{2}$ inch from each end of the suede patch. The cuts should straddle the imaginary centerline of the piece. See image **a**.

7 Push 2 inches of surgical tubing (using the ends that don't have the poly tubing inserted in them) through each slit. Push through from the smooth side to the rough side. We'll use the rough side of the suede to give us a better grip on the things we want to sling.

8 Fold the surgical tubing back over itself, pinching the suede in between the two halves of the fold. Cut an 18-inch piece of nylon string and use it to tightly whip the two pieces of tubing together. (See **Whipping, Steps 1–4**.) Do the same for the other side.

9 Cut an 8-inch piece of athletic tape and rip it down the middle lengthwise. Take one piece and wrap it tightly around the whipping on one side. Do the same with the other piece on the other side.

10 Grab the stick and, with the pocketknife, cut a ¾-inch notch into the back side of each arm, ½ inch down from the top. See image **b**. The back side is the part that will be facing away from you when you fire the slingshot.

11 Now we're going to attach the surgical tubing—the ends with the poly inserts—to the arms of the stick. Lay the tubing lengthwise exactly along the front of each arm so the tubing and stick overlap 2 inches. Add a wrap of athletic tape to each side to hold the surgical tubing in place.

12 Tightly whip the tubing onto the arm. Start the first wrap of the whipping in the notch you made in Step 10, and be sure to make the wraps very tight. This is an important step that, if done right, will ensure the strength of the slingshot.

13 On both arms, add some glue down the length of the whipping, pressing it down into the nylon. See image **c**.

14 Wrap athletic tape very tightly around the arms to cover all of the whipping.

15 Now test it. Grab a marble and go pop a tin can. Watch it zing! Brings back memories, huh?

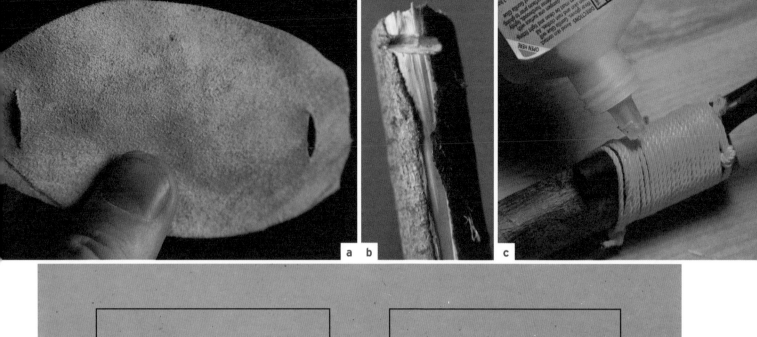

a b c

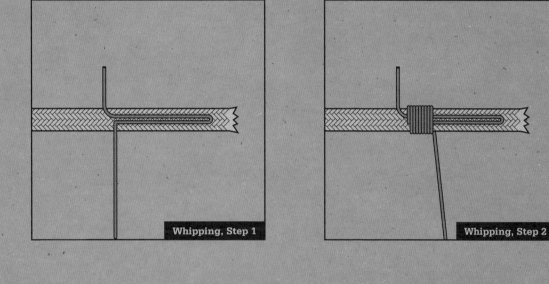

Whipping, Step 1

Whipping, Step 2

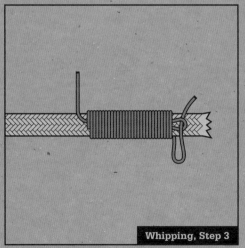

Whipping, Step 3

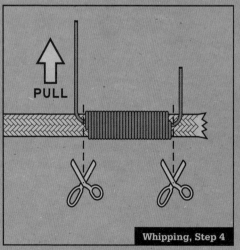

PULL

Whipping, Step 4

WATER-BALLOON LAUNCHER

Are you aware that sneak attacks on tree forts and back-yard bases rise dramatically in the summertime? Are your kids concerned that their backyard hideaways are vulnerable? In situations like these, I recommend that responsible parents provide their children with water balloon–based defensive systems like the launcher described here. Kids in teams of three can repel would-be attackers quite effectively. Then again, you could play the double agent and provide these plans to your neighbor to make for his kids. Then the two of you can sit on your deck with the cold beverages of your choice and watch the fracas ensue. Don't forget to provide the water balloons.

DIFFICULTY LEVEL:
Challenging

TIME INVOLVED:
An afternoon

MATERIALS:

24 feet ⁷⁄₁₆- to ½-inch silicone surgical tubing
(Available online at reefscuba.com.)

1 foot ¾-inch clear PVC tubing

2 feet ³⁄₁₆-inch thermostat wire

18 inches ¼-inch thermostat wire

One 6-inch plastic funnel

FASTENERS:

Strong duct tape (1 roll)

Athletic tape (1 roll)

TOOLS:

Scissors

Drill with ³⁄₁₆-inch and ¼-inch bits

NOTE: For details on tying the knots referred to in this project, refer to the Knots section on page 162.

1 Use the scissors to cut the surgical tubing into two equal pieces.

2 Cut the clear PVC tubing into two equal pieces and thread a piece of surgical tubing through each piece.

3 Create a closed loop out of each piece of surgical tubing by tying the ends together using a square knot. Leave a tail end of about 3 inches of tubing on each side of the knot. See the Knots section (pg. 162) for details.

4 Using a piece of athletic tape, attach the tail ends to the surgical-tubing loop on both sides of the knot. Then wrap the entire knot, from tail end to tail end, in athletic tape to form a grip. Do the same thing with the other loop of surgical tubing. You should now have two large loops of surgical tubing, each with a grip and a section of clear tube. See image **a**.

5 Grab the funnel and drill two 3⁄16-inch holes, 1 inch apart and ½ inch down from the wide-end rim. Drill two holes in the same position on the exact opposite side of the funnel. See image **b**.

6 Cut the 3⁄16-inch thermostat wire into two equal pieces and run each piece through the holes you drilled in each side of the funnel. Thread the wire so that its tail ends poke out through the exterior of the funnel. See image **c**.

7 Now, using the thermostat wire, tie the funnel to the large loop at the midpoint of the PVC tubing. Tie it with a square knot so that wire forms a 2-inch diameter ring. Wrap the tail ends of the knot completely around the ring. Do the same with the other loop on the other side of the funnel. See image **d**.

8 Tear an 8-inch piece of duct tape in half lengthwise and wrap one half around one of the wire loops. You want to hold the wire down and reinforce it, so really smash down the tape to create a thick, solid ring. Do the same on the other side.

9 Move the grip on the large loop so that it's exactly opposite the clear PVC tubing. Then make sure the wire ring is exactly in the middle of the PVC tubing. When that's all lined up, pinch the PVC in half, catching the wire ring in the fold. Secure the PVC with athletic tape. See images **e** and **f**.

10 Now wrap the entire PVC/wire ring joint very tightly with athletic tape. Cover all of the duct tape and continue wrapping up the PVC to within 1⁄8 inch of the end. See image **g**. Repeat Steps 9 and 10 for the other side of the funnel.

11 Drill a ¼-inch hole through the funnel's spout, 1 inch from the tip, so you end up with a hole on both sides of the spout. Imagine a line connecting the holes on the rim of the funnel, and drill this hole perpendicular to that line. See image **h**.

12 Thread the ¼-inch thermostat wire through both ¼-inch holes and, without tying the ends together, make a 3½-inch-wide loop. Wrap this loop tightly with athletic tape, starting and finishing just beyond the points where the ends overlap. See image **i**.

13 Now grab a few water balloons and enlist some combination of kids and/or kids' friends to form a team of three. You'll need two kids to hold the grips (one kid per grip) and one to launch the balloons. Have the grip holders stretch out their arms in the direction of the balloon's flight and brace themselves. The third kid will load the funnel, pull it taut, aim, and fire.

There you go! Your children's fort defenses are organized. Now grab that beverage and rendezvous with your fellow double agent to watch the action!

a

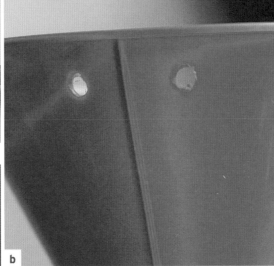

b

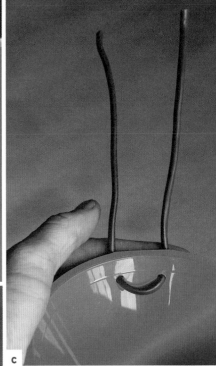

c

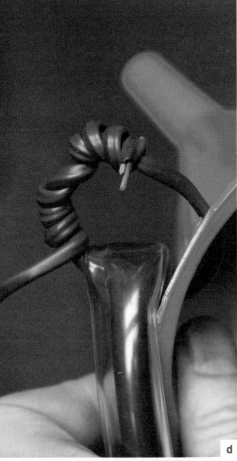

d

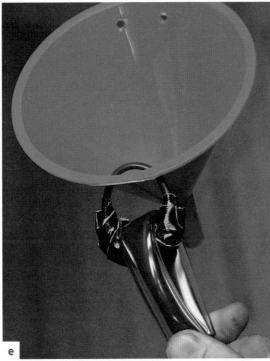

e

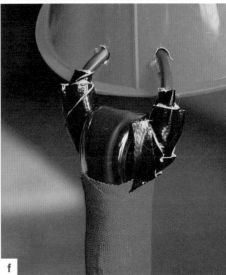

f

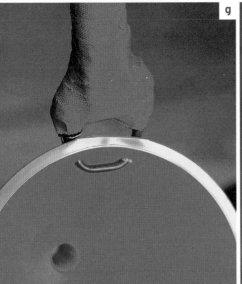

g

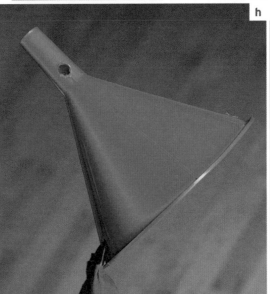

h

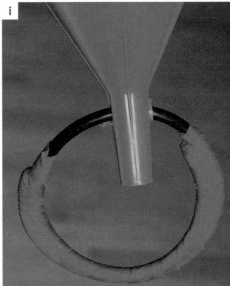

i

BIRD FEEDER

Everyone loves a good roadside restaurant. As they head south, why not give our feathered friends the same pleasure? This bird feeder works in any environment. It has a huge capacity for seed storage, so you won't have to spend a lot of time refilling. The untreated redwood will fade beautifully as it ages, lasting for many years. I built one with a pitched roof, which allows the rain to roll off and protects the seed from the elements. It also ensures that the birds can't park up there and mess up the food. The single hook makes for easy removal and refilling, and also makes it difficult for crafty squirrels or chipmunks to climb up and dine-and-dash. If birds had travel guides, this feeder would get five stars!

DIFFICULTY LEVEL:
Challenging

TIME INVOLVED:
An afternoon

MATERIALS:

Two 6-foot 1×8 redwood fence boards. (You may also use S4S lumber, which is sanded on four sides.)

¼-×-6-inch wooden dowel

FASTENERS:

2-inch wood screws (21)

1¼-inch wood screws (2)

3-inch wood screw (1)

TOOLS:

Circular saw

Drill with ¼-inch drill bit and 1-inch spade bit

Utility knife

Pencil

Wood glue

AND ...

One 15-pound sack of high-quality millet. Don't substitute greasy-spoon feed here!

Note: We'll be cutting nine pieces of wood out of our two fence boards, leaving almost no waste; measure and cut carefully! Consult the illustration for guidance on your cuts. See **Bird Feeder Board Cutting Guide.**

INSTRUCTIONS:

1 Measure 7 inches from the end of one of the fence boards, set the miter on your circular saw to 45°, and make a beveled cut, as shown in image **a**. Label this piece **INTERNAL RAMP**.

2 Turn the same board over and measure 12½ inches from the tip of the beveled edge, set the miter back to 0, and make a straight cut. Label this piece **FRONT** on its longer face, which will be on the inside of the feeder when it is assembled.

3 Measure 21½ inches from one end of the board and make another cut. Label this piece **ROOF**.

4 You should be left with a board that is about 28 inches long. Set your saw's miter to 20° and trim off one edge of the board, preserving as much of its length as you can. Label this piece **BACK** on the face that is slightly longer, which will end up on the inside of the assembled feeder.

5 Turn the **BACK** piece over so you're looking at what will be the outside-facing side. From the non-beveled edge, draw a line about 4 inches long down the center of the board. Put a mark at 3 inches and another at 3½ inches.

6 Now we'll drill some holes. Place the board on some scrap wood so the drill bits don't make splinters when they come through the other side. Drill a ¼-inch hole at the 3-inch mark, and use a spade bit to drill a 1-inch hole at the 3½-inch mark. These two holes will overlap to form a single keyhole shape, from which the feeder will hang.

7 Take the other fence board and cut off a 2½-inch piece and label it **INTERNAL ROOF BLOCK**. Cut a 3¾-inch piece and label it **LOWER FRONT**. Cut a 6-inch piece and label it **BOTTOM**. Cut the remaining piece in half—you should end up with two pieces that each are about 29½ inches long. You will cut the sidewalls out of these pieces.

8 Enlarge the **Bird Feeder Sides Template** by 500 percent. Cut it out with a utility knife and ruler, then use a pencil to trace the pattern onto the two remaining pieces of board and cut out the **SIDEWALLS**. You should now have all the pieces shown in the photo. See image **b**.

9 Okay, let's start assembling. Lay the **BACK** down on your work surface with the inside face facing up. Now put the **SIDEWALLS** into position so that their pointed ends are on the same end of the bird feeder as the keyhole. Making sure the sidewalls are flush with the edge of the **BACK**, use three 2-inch wood screws per side to attach the sidewalls to its inside face.

10 Using two 2-inch screws per side, attach the **BOTTOM** piece to the bottom edges of the **SIDEWALLS**. See image **c**.

11 Attach the **LOWER FRONT** piece to the lower, front-facing portion on the **SIDEWALLS** using two 2-inch screws per side.

12 Find the piece labeled **INTERNAL RAMP**. Trim its width from 8 inches to 6 inches so it measures 6 × 7 inches. Now slide it into the bottom of the bird feeder so that the 45° beveled edge is flush against the back wall. Secure it to the back wall using two 2-inch wood screws. See image **d**.

13 Find the piece labeled **FRONT**. This will form the front wall of the feeder, just above the feeding trough. Lay it across the edges of the **SIDEWALLS** so the 45° beveled edge is facing up. This beveled edge should line up with the top edges of the sidewalls to form the opening at the top of the feeder. Make sure everything is flush and attach this piece to the sidewalls using four 2-inch wood screws. See image **e**.

14 Find the **INTERNAL ROOF BLOCK** and trim it from 2½ × 8 inches to 2½ × 6 inches.

15 Now we're going to mount the **INTERNAL ROOF BLOCK** so it acts as a stop to keep the **ROOF** from sliding off of the feeder. Lay the bird feeder on its back on a level surface. Find the **ROOF**, lay it flush over the top opening of the feeder, and let it slide down until it touches your work surface. Now, without moving it up or down, slide the roof sideways until the opening of the bird feeder is exposed. Mark the side of the roof where it meets the inside edge of the **FRONT**. Transfer this line to the inside of the **ROOF**. Using the two 1¼-inch screws, mount the **INTERNAL ROOF BLOCK** so that it butts up against this line. It should be centered width-wise and will end up on the inside of the feeder when mounted. See image **f**.

16 Use a 2-inch wood screw to secure the upper left-hand corner of the roof panel. You'll unscrew this when it's time to refill.

17 Lay the bird feeder on its back again and drill a ¼-inch hole in the middle of the lower front panel. Drill through the **LOWER FRONT** panel and **INTERNAL RAMP**, but don't drill through the rear of the feeder. Make sure this hole is perpendicular to the back face of the feeder so the landing perch is parallel to the ground when the feeder is mounted. See image **g**.

18 Drip some wood glue into the hole and insert the ¼-inch wooden dowel. This will support even the chubbiest of birdseed enthusiasts.

19 Find a sturdy, visible spot outside your window. Screw the 3-inch wood screw into your mounting location and hang the feeder. Fill it with the millet and watch the birds make a beeline to their new hotspot.

g

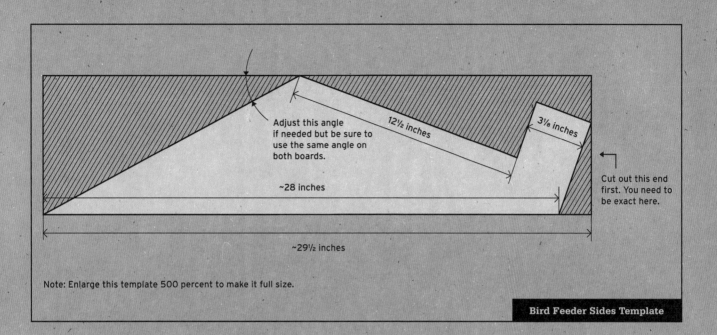

Adjust this angle if needed but be sure to use the same angle on both boards.

12½ inches

3⅛ inches

~28 inches

Cut out this end first. You need to be exact here.

~29½ inches

Note: Enlarge this template 500 percent to make it full size.

Bird Feeder Sides Template

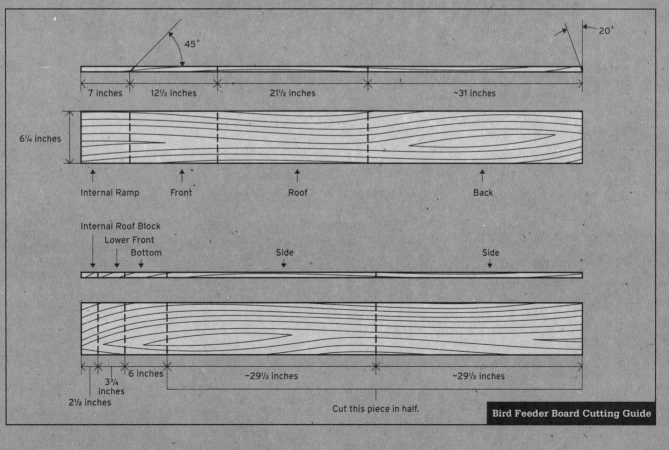

45°

20°

7 inches

12½ inches

21½ inches

~31 inches

6¼ inches

Internal Ramp

Front

Roof

Back

Internal Roof Block

Lower Front

Bottom

Side

Side

6 inches

~29½ inches

~29½ inches

3¾ inches

2½ inches

Cut this piece in half.

Bird Feeder Board Cutting Guide

SAND CANDLES

Candles are always nice. They smell good, create a pleasant ambience, and—your kids might be interested in knowing—can be given to cute girls or boys as gifts. The possibilities for making candle are endless. You can use different colors of wax, layer colors together, combine patterns, and add scents, glitter, or anything else. How about adding some foreign coins to make a money candle? Who knows—it might bring good fortune when lit.

DIFFICULTY LEVEL:
Challenging

TIME INVOLVED:
An afternoon

MATERIALS:

Clean sand (enough to fill half a 5-gallon bucket)

Three bricks beeswax or scented candle wax

Three candle wicks (usually included with the wax brick—but double-check to be sure)

OPTIONAL ITEMS:

Ammonite or amethyst in various sizes

Glitter

Candle oils, to add custom scents

TOOLS:

Three large bowls (about 3 quarts each)

Camping stove

Two 9-inch foil pie pans

Wet towel, to throw over any errant sparks or flames

Medium saucepan, with a handle and a notched lip for pouring (You can also bend a notch into an old saucepan yourself.)

Cup, mug, and/or shot glass, to be the pattern for the mold

Ten wooden kebab skewers

Metal spoon

1. Fill the three large bowls three-quarters full with sand. This will be the basis for the mold.

2. To figure out if the sand is wet enough to hold a shape, press your fist into the sand and slowly remove it. If the sand retains the imprint of your fist, the water content is fine. If it doesn't, mix some water (approximately 1 cup) into the sand until it does—the drier the sand, the thicker the sand coating on the outside of the candles. You can tune this to your preference.

3. Alright, now let's set up the camping stove. Place the burner in a pie tin to protect your work surface from the heat. See image **a**. Light the stove and adjust it to medium heat. Keep the wet towel nearby.

4. Drop a piece of wax brick into the saucepan and place the pan on the stove—how much depends on the molds. See image **b**. This first pour should fill all of the molds halfway up. While that's melting, let's make our first mold.

5. We'll start with a simple one. Push the cup, mug, or shot glass (whatever you're using as a pattern) down into the sand to a depth of 2 to 4 inches, depending on how long the wick is. See image **c**. If you have longer wicks, you may press the pattern deeper into the sand. Whatever the length, the wick should stand at least ½ inch above the surface of the sand.

6. Pull the pattern out (see image **d**) and break the skewers in half and keep them handy. These will support the wick once we pour.

7. To make extra-cool candles, incorporate the ammonite or amethyst. Press it into the sand, with the crystals toward the middle of the bowl. If one end of the geode is wider than the other, keep the wider end on the bottom for stability. Press it into the sand and press a mug in right next to it. See image **e**. The depth of both the mug and the geode should be the same, and one-half to two-thirds of the geode should be standing above the surface of the sand. Pull out the mug and the mold is ready. See image **f**.

8. Try something experimental in the third mold. For mine, I used the same pattern three times to make a complex shape and added some glitter. See image **g**. Is the wax melted yet? How about now? Will it be enough to fill all of the molds half full? If not, add a little more.

9. Here's how this will work. You'll slowly pour the wax over the metal spoon, keeping both it and the lip of the saucepan very close to the void in the mold. This will prevent the pouring wax from eroding the sand walls. If using, add your scented oil before pouring. Okay, ready? Go ahead and pour, filling about half the void of each mold. See image **h**.

10. Place a wick into the wax at what will be the center bottom of each candle. Support the top of the wick with half of a skewer placed on top of the sand. If that doesn't quite work for some reason, place two skewers in an X and place the end of the wick right where the two skewers cross. That will hold it for sure. See image **i**.

11. Melt another batch of wax (enough to fill up all the molds) and let it cool for a couple of minutes before you pour so that you won't melt the wax that's already hardened in the molds. Using your metal spoon, pour all three molds.

12. Now start to melt another small, third batch. When the wax solidifies it tends to sink and settle a little bit in the molds (see image **j**), so this last batch is just to fill in the sinks so that the candles look smooth on the top. When the third pour is ready, go ahead and fill in the tops.

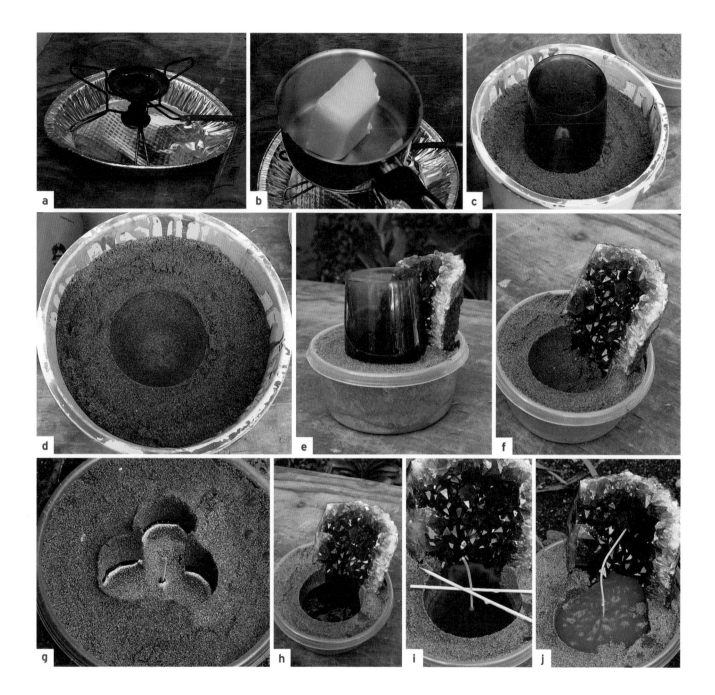

13 After about a half hour, the candles will have cooled to a point that you can dig them out of the sand. Do this when they're ready, brushing off the excess sand.

14 If your candles have round bottoms, heat the pan again and melt a flat base onto the bottom of each candle.

15 Now we're into the finishing touches. Break off any uneven pieces from the upper edges and rinse each candle with water to get rid of any lingering sand.

16 When you're ready, light it and watch whatever magic you added come to life!

ANGEL WINGS

Who wouldn't want to fly through their dreams on these graceful wings? Whether for angel, eagle, fairy princess, or Pegasus, nothing beats soaring through the night on magical wings of fur and feathers (with a little help from Dad, of course). Yes, if you please, with wings such as these, there's no telling the places they'll see.

A note on color: we recommend white for angel and Pegasus wings (as in the instructions below), brown for eagle feathers, and pink for fairy princess gear. Or mix it up and let your imagination run wild!

DIFFICULTY LEVEL:
Challenging

TIME INVOLVED:
An afternoon

MATERIALS:

¾-inch sheet sound-deadening board, 4 × 8 feet

¼-inch sheet Masonite, 4 × 8 feet

2 yards thick faux-fur fabric (very fluffy), white

1 yard thin faux-fur fabric (slightly fluffy), white

Bleached turkey feathers (125 count), white or any color you desire

FASTENERS:

⅛-×-1-inch machine nuts and bolts (4)

Heavy-duty ½-inch staples

TOOLS:

Black permanent marker

Jigsaw with multipurpose blade

White spray paint

Drill with ⅛-inch bit

Heavy-duty stapler that can handle ½-inch staples

1 Create an angel wing template following the **OUTER WING** diagram on page 66. Enlarge the diagram by blowing it up 800 percent to make a 48-inch template. Place it on the ¾-inch sound-deadening board.

2 Trace the shape of the template onto the sound-deadening board with your marker.

3 Cut out the wing with your jigsaw (see image **a**) and label this piece **OUTER RIGHT**.

4 Lay the **OUTER RIGHT** wing facedown onto the remaining ¾-inch sound-deadening board and trace it with your marker.

5 Grab your jigsaw again and cut out this wing along your marker line and label it **OUTER LEFT**.

6 Lay out the wings so there is a right and left wing. Spray paint the "fingers" on the front sides of both wings white.

7 Repeat Steps 1 through 5 using the **INNER WING** diagram, this time substituting Masonite for sound-deadening board and labeling the two wings **INNER RIGHT** and **INNER LEFT**.

8 Position the inner wing pieces on top of the outer wing pieces, making sure the wings are positioned similarly in both left and right sets. See image **b**.

9 Starting with the right-hand set of wings, drill two ⅛-inch holes all the way through both the inner and outer wings. (Put some scrap board under the outer wing so you don't drill a hole into your work surface.) Space the holes pretty far apart, but don't drill too close to the edges of the inner wing. See image **c**. Repeat for the left-hand set of wings.

10 Place the outer wings onto the thick faux-fur fabric. Make sure they're oriented so you'll end up with both right- and left-hand pieces when you trace them (i.e.,

they should be pointing in opposite directions). Good? Okay. Now trace both outer wings with a solid line around the fingers, and a dashed line around the top edges where there are no fingers. Now cut out the fabric on the solid trace line, but leave 2 inches of extra fabric around the dotted lines. We'll fold this extra fabric over the wing later and staple it down.

11 Grab the outer wings and, matching the curve of the feathers to the curve of the fingers, staple 5 to 7 turkey feathers to each finger, staggering them and making sure each feather extends ½ inch or so beyond the edge of the sound-deadening board. See image **d**.

12 Lay the thick faux-fur fabric over the outer wing on the same side as the feathers. Line up the fabric and tack it to the wing at the base of every other finger. Turn the wing over. Pull the extra 2 inches of fabric taut, fold it over the back of the wing, and staple it down. Repeat this step with the other wing.

13 Turn the outer wings back over so the fur is on top, and trim back the fur that's covering the now-feathered fingers. The idea is to let more of the feathers show, but to leave enough fabric to cover the quills.

14 Get the inner wings and place them onto the thin faux-fur fabric. Again, make sure they're lying down as a left and right wing. Trace a solid line about 2 inches around the edge of each wing—you want to end up with fabric pieces that are bigger than the wings themselves. Draw a dashed line around the Masonite itself. This will help you orient the pieces later.

15 Place the bolts through the holes in the inner wings and screw on the nuts. You're going to bolt these to the outer wing, so again make sure you have left- and right-hand pieces. Still good? Okay, now line up the inner wings with the dotted lines you drew on the thin faux-fur pieces,

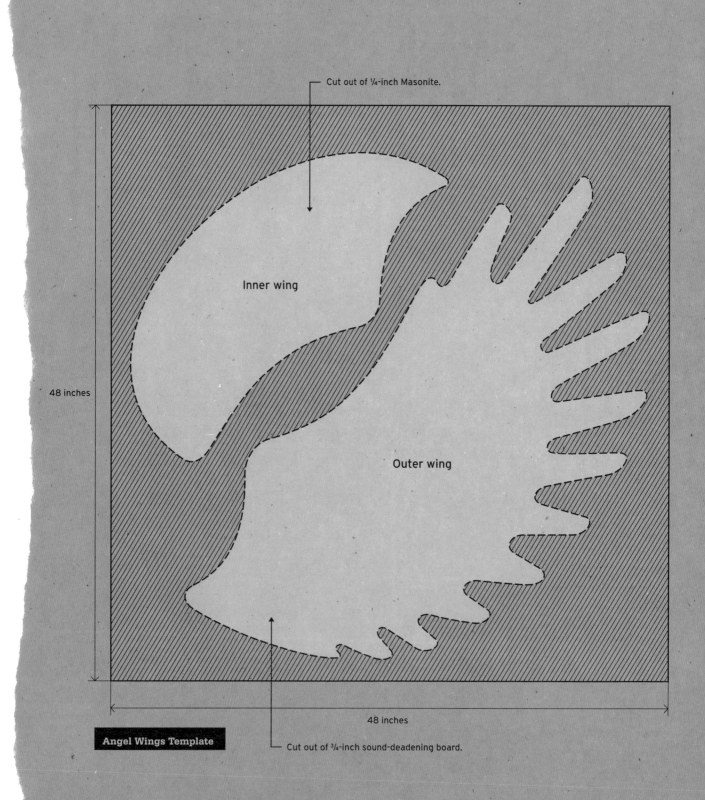

Cut out of ¼-inch Masonite.

Inner wing

Outer wing

48 inches

48 inches

Angel Wings Template

Cut out of ¾-inch sound-deadening board.

so the fabric covers the heads of the bolts. Fold the excess fabric over the back of the inner wing and staple it down. Tack it first in four or six places and then work your way around. Repeat with the other inner wing.

16 Now unscrew the nuts from the inner wings and line up the bolts with the holes on the fur side of the outer wings. When you can feel that they're lined up, press the bolts through the thick fur and screw the nuts back on to connect the inner and outer wings.

17 Hang the wings as you would two pictures on a wall, keeping them about 3 inches apart at the middle.

Let your kids' dreams take flight.

CLIMBING WALL

You know what's good fun? Bouldering. Picking the perfect path and clawing your way to the top of a huge rock satisfies like not much else. It's one of my favorite things about camping. Not long after I've pitched the tent, you'll find me whooping it up atop some big boulder. And bigger boulders = bigger fun! But not everyone has Half Dome in their backyard. So what do you do? Build your kids a climbing wall! All it takes are some handholds and a trip to the hardware store.

DIFFICULTY LEVEL:
Challenging

TIME INVOLVED:
An afternoon

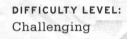

MATERIALS:

A huge tree (If you don't have one handy, you can mount the wall on the side of your house.)

1½-inch plywood subflooring (one 4×8 sheet)

1 quart exterior house paint that blends well with the chosen environment

One 8-foot 2×6 Douglas fir board

Two 16-foot 2×6 Douglas fir boards

About 40 synthetic handholds
(These can be ordered from outdoor-equipment stores in packages that include hardware. See Resources, pg. 165.)

OPTIONAL:

Cowbell, for ringing when your kids make it to the top

FASTENERS:

½-×-10-inch lag bolts with washers (6)

3-inch wood screws (50-count box)

TOOLS:

Circular saw

Drill with Phillips-head bit and ¼-×-12-inch and ⅜-inch bits

Ladder

Level

½-inch socket wrench

Allen wrench, to attach the handholds (usually included)

INSTRUCTIONS:

1 Trim any branches, up to 16 feet high, that would prevent you from attaching the climbing wall to your tree.

2 With the circular saw, cut the subflooring down the middle lengthwise to make two equal 2-×-8-foot pieces.

3 Paint the smoother sides of the two pieces with the house paint you've picked. Don't forget the edges, but don't worry about the back side. Now watch the paint dry. Just kidding—that'd be about as exciting as watching . . . never mind.

4 Now we'll make the supports. Cut the 8-foot 2×6 board into four 2-foot pieces. We'll need only three of them. Save the last one to make shims, in case you need them in Step 8.

5 Into each of the three pieces you've just cut, drill two ¼-inch holes. The holes should be centered on the board and at least 6 inches apart. See image **a**.

6 Hold one of these boards level (using the level) on the horizontal and centered against the tree about a foot off the ground and use it as a drilling template. Do this by placing the bit in each hole and drilling an inch or so into the tree.

7 Remove the board and, again keeping the drill level, deepen each hole to a depth of about 6 inches.

8 Now attach the lower support to the tree using the 10-inch lag bolts and washers. Since most trees are round, you'll probably need to put shims behind the board to ensure a good fit. Drill holes in the shims too. Now attach the board to the tree. See images **b** and **c**.

9 Now let's attach the middle and upper supports the same way. Grab your ladder and position it near the tree. You might want to throw some wide scrap boards under the legs if the ground is soft, so they don't sink in. The distance from the top edge of the upper support to the bottom edge of the lower support should be 16 feet. That's the

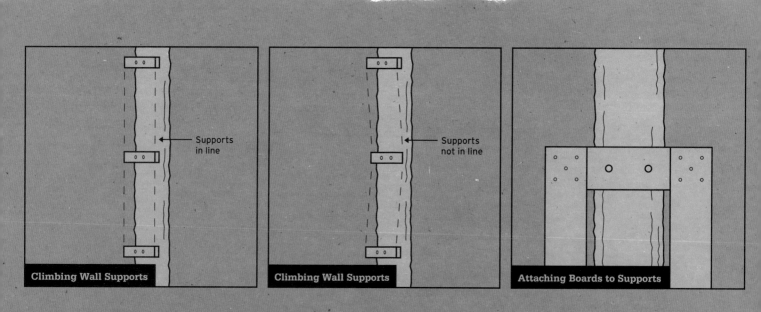

Supports in line

Climbing Wall Supports

Supports not in line

Climbing Wall Supports

Attaching Boards to Supports

same length as the beam we'll be supporting. The middle support should be exactly halfway between the other two, that is, 8 feet on center from either the bottom of the lower or the top of the upper supports. When attaching the supports, make sure they're all in the same plane. To do this, mount the supports temporarily with a couple wood screws and lean the 16-foot boards against them and see how things look. See **Climbing Wall Supports**.

10 Now mount the 16-foot 2×6 boards vertically so they're flush with the outer edges of the supports, one on the left, one on the right. Attach the boards to each support using five wood screws in a cross pattern (like the 5 on a pair of dice). I used two 8-foot boards in the photo, but I'm spec'ing 16-footers here. See image **d** and **Attaching Boards to Supports**.

11 Attach 20 of the mountaineering handholds to each of the pieces of sub-flooring, ensuring that they're about 18 to 24 inches apart from one another, and that the biggest surface area on each one is facing up. Drill a

⅜-inch hole where you'd like to put each one, and screw it down using the Allen wrench and the included hardware. (Speaking of hardware, the size of the hole you need to drill may vary depending on the hardware that came with the handholds.) Later on, if you'd like, you can loosen the handholds and turn them upside down if your kids need a bigger challenge. See images **e** and **f**.

12 Mount the first piece of the climbing wall to the vertical 2×6 supports. It should fit flush with their outside edges. Attach using wood screws every 6 inches, and 2 inches from the edge.

13 Mount the second half of the wall in the same way. Call in support from a friend or neighbor to make this part of the job easier.

14 As a final touch, mount a cowbell to the top of the wall. It'll be fun for your kids to ring that thing and let everyone know they scaled to the summit. Next stop, Half Dome!

WEEKEND
PROJECTS

SKATE LONGBOARD

Have you ever noticed how many roads there are in your neck of the woods? Everywhere you look, there are smooth, sloping asphalt waves—I mean, slopes—just waiting to be carved up. Get into a crouch or put your toes on the nose. Feel the flow as you—I mean, your kids—carve back and forth across the blacktop with the sun on their faces and the wind in their hair. Actually, let's not kid ourselves. I have a feeling you're going be "borrowing" this board to relive those early glory days of skateboarding yourself.

DIFFICULTY LEVEL:
Challenging

TIME INVOLVED:
A weekend

MATERIALS:

4-foot 1×7 Brazilian Ipe wood* (This sounds like an odd size but it's actually a factory-cut measurement. Look for Ipe wood at your local specialty lumberyard.)

2 super-wide 10-inch skateboard trucks
(I like Independent-brand trucks, myself.)

One set of super-soft street wheels
(Yup, they come 4 to a set.)

Eight bearings built for speed

4 feet clear grip tape, 10 inches wide

FASTENERS:

1½-inch skateboard mounting hardware, for bolting the trucks to the deck

* *A quick note about Ipe wood: It's an incredibly strong, dense wood that's resistant to splintering and nicking, which makes it super-durable for daily use. It's pretty weatherproof too, naturally resisting rot, decay, insects, and mold. Sunlight has little to no effect on its structural integrity, but it will eventually transform from its original reddish-brown color to a beautiful silver patina. What's more, Ipe wood is an environmentally responsible choice because it's harvested only from sustainable sources. It's also naturally fire-resistant, which I know will come in handy when you—whoops, I mean your kids—are heating up the street on their new deck.*

TOOLS:

Measuring tape

4-foot level or straightedge

Pencil

Carpenter's square

Felt-tip pen

Drill with ³⁄₁₆-inch and ¼-inch bits

Band saw or jigsaw with wood blade

Electric sander with a few sheets of 60-grit sand paper

Screwdriver

Utility knife or pocketknife

Socket wrench with ½-inch, ³⁄₈-inch, and ⁹⁄₁₆-inch sockets

1 Look your board over and find an area that has the most attractive grain. We'll make this the nose (top) of the board. Now turn the board over—we'll be making all our marks on this side, which will be the underside.

2 Draw a centerline lengthwise on the board: use the measuring tape to measure 3½ inches from the edge and use your level and pencil to make a clean straight line.

3 Now we're going to start laying out the shape of the deck. This will be the beautiful, classic teardrop shape known as a "pin tail." This board, in Ipe wood, will look just as amazing carving down the street as it will when you get it home and hang it on your wall. Measure 1 inch from the nose edge and draw a line horizontally across the board with your carpenter's square. You may want to label this and the following marks with the measurements as you go, because you'll need to refer back to them. See **Marking the Curve of the Deck.**

4 Draw another horizontal line at 2 inches from the nose edge, one at 3½ inches, one at 5½ inches, and another at 12 inches. See images **a** and **b**.

5 Now, measuring from the long sides of the board, we'll make marks across these lines. When we're done with these steps, we should have a set of perfectly symmetrical marks on our board. Start by crossing the 1-inch line at points 2¼ inches from each edge. See images **c** and **d**.

6 Cross the 2-inch horizontal line at points 1½ inches from the outside edges. See images **c** and **d**.

7 Cross the 3½-inch horizontal line at points 1 inch from the outside edges. See images **c** and **d**.

8 Cross the 5½-inch horizontal line at points ½ inch from the outside edges.

9 And finally, at the 12-inch horizontal line, make a mark right on the outside edges.

10 Okay, that's it for the front section. We'll make some more horizontal lines now, for the tail shape. The first one will be 28 inches from the nose.

11 Draw another horizontal line at 35¼ inches, one at 40½ inches, one at 44½ inches, and another at 47 inches.

12 Great. Now cross the 28-inch line ½ inch from each edge.

13 Now cross the 35¼-inch horizontal line 1 inch from both outside edges.

14 Cross the 40½-inch horizontal line at points 1½ inches from the outside edges.

15 Cross the 44½-inch horizontal line at points 2 inches from the outside edges.

16 Cross the 47-inch horizontal line at points 2½ inches from the outside edges.

17 Now we'll connect all of these points with a long, smooth freehand curve to form the pin-back shape of our deck. With your pencil, sketch out one curve. When you do the curve on the other side, make sure it looks exactly identical. Both curves should meet the edge of the board at the 12-inch horizontal line—this will be the widest part of the deck. Since most of your—whoops, I did it again—your kid's weight will be on his front foot when he pulls heavy G's through the turns, this part has to be beefy.

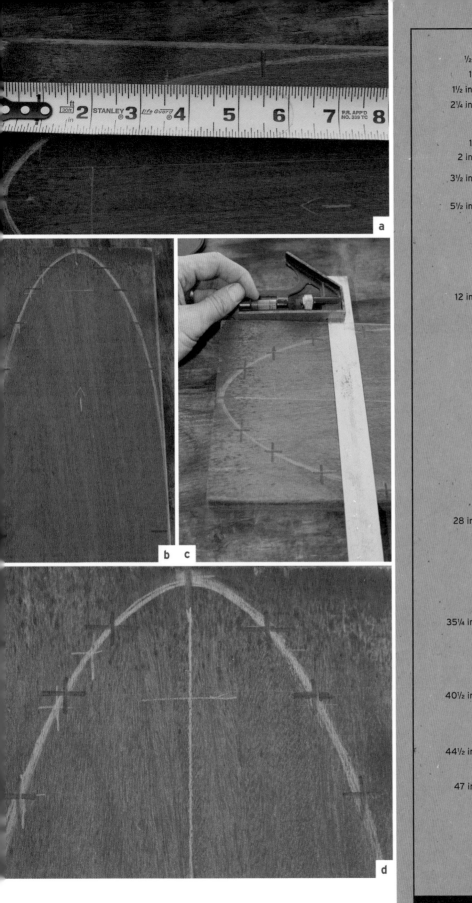

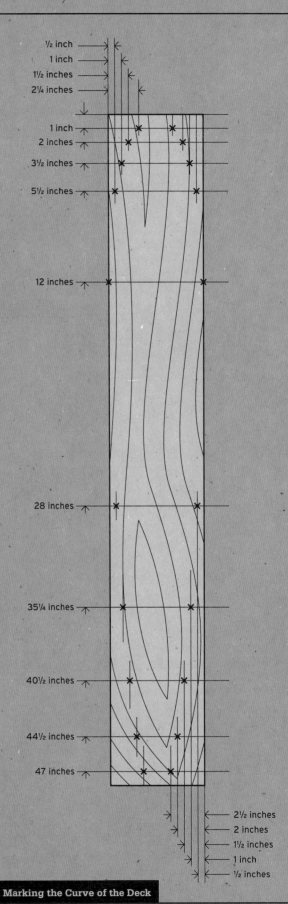

½ inch

1 inch

1½ inches

2¼ inches

1 inch

2 inches

3½ inches

5½ inches

12 inches

28 inches

35¼ inches

40½ inches

44½ inches

47 inches

2½ inches

2 inches

1½ inches

1 inch

½ inches

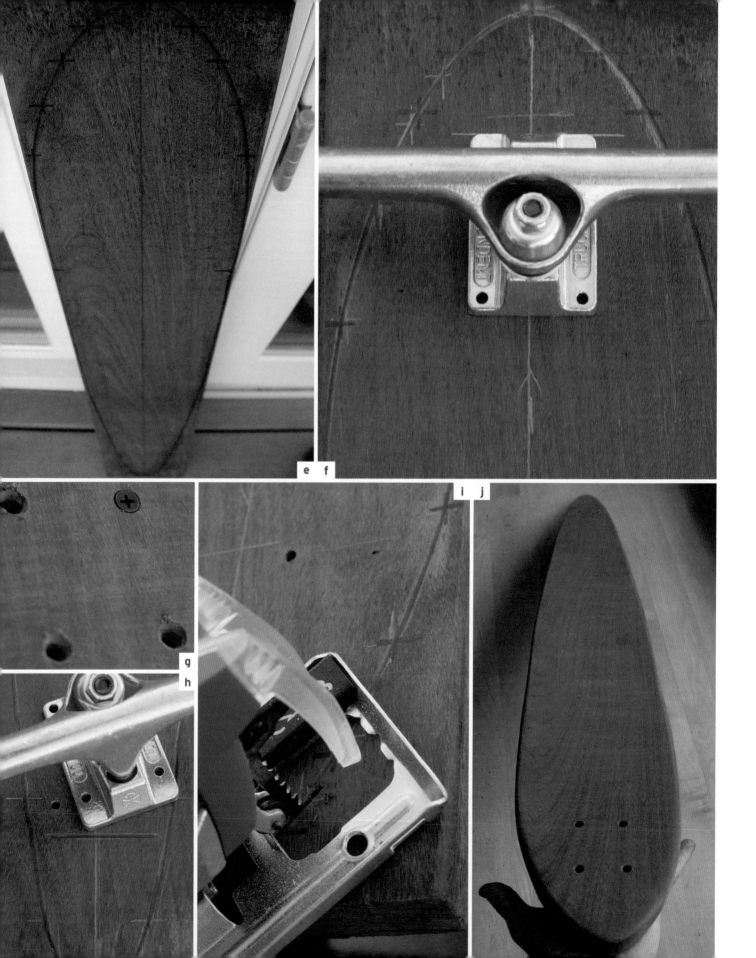

e f

g

h

i j

18 Okay, let's continue the curve through the tail section. Follow the edge of the board from the 12-inch horizontal in an almost-straight line. When you get about two-thirds of the way to the 28½-inch horizontal, start to curve in toward it.

19 Carefully connect all the rest of the crossed points.

20 To complete the tail, go right to the end of the board and connect the two lines with a half circle.

21 Now go back over the layout of your curves and make sure all the transitions from point to point are smooth. The best way to do this is to sight down the length of your board. How do things look? Take a moment here to tune in to the board. There aren't a lot of handmade decks out there, so savor your contribution to the art of board shaping. Soak up the sights and smells, and let it flow. See image **e**.

22 So, do you have a sweet-looking curve on your board? Great! Now carefully trace it with your felt-tip pen so it's easier to see when you cut it with the jigsaw.

23 Before we cut, though, let's predrill the holes for the trucks. Draw a horizontal line on the underside of the board 2 inches from the nose with the carpenter's square.

24 Now get your drill and the ³⁄₁₆-inch bit ready. Place one of the trucks on the centerline so the front of it is flush with the 2-inch line and the king pin and rubber bushing is facing the middle of the board. Truck placement has to be dead-on and level along the centerline of the board, so be sure to be accurate here. If the trucks are out of alignment, the board will want to go in two directions at once. Two directions on one board = bad idea. See image **f**.

25 Is everything lined up? OK. Hold the truck down firmly and, using the pencil, trace the position of each hole onto the deck. Now measure the positions of each hole on the truck, i.e., the distance of the center of each hole from the front edge and from the centerline. Using your carpenter's square, double check that the holes you marked on the deck match the measurements you just made. Drill four pilot holes, one through the center of each hole in the truck.

26 If everything looks good, remove the truck. Now place the board on a smooth scrap-wood surface and, using the same ³⁄₁₆-inch bit, drill the holes for the trucks all the way through the board. Make sure to hold the board down firmly so you don't splinter the wood when the drill comes through the other side.

27 So that you—whoops . . . oh, never mind—don't feel the screw heads as you're carving the asphalt jungle, let's make some countersinks on the topside of the deck. To do this, use a ¼-inch bit and put the drill into reverse. Put the bit in one of the holes and start the drill. Now rotate in a circle as you tilt the drill about 45°. Practice on a scrap piece of wood first if you like. Don't forget to put the drill in reverse so you don't gouge your deck. See image **g**.

28 Make another line 3 inches from the tail of the board and repeat the same process down there with the other truck. Putting the rear truck forward by an inch makes for a stronger connection, since the board will be pretty thin at that end. Again, make sure the kingpin and bushing are facing the middle of the board and that the back edge of the truck is flush on the 3-inch line. See image **h**.

29 Alright, let's free the skateboard from the block of wood it's trapped in. A band saw is really ideal for this, but a jigsaw will work well too. Take your time and follow the line exactly. If you feel an error coming on, make it on the outside of the line. Or give your self a little breathing room and cut a hair outside of the line. You can always sand it down, but you can't put wood back. Start all your cuts from the nose and tail, cutting toward the 12-inch mark. See image **i**.

30 Great! Your deck is free! Now it's sanding time. This step will take 45 minutes to an hour. Start by sanding down the sawn edge so it's flush with the curves you laid out, making any rookie sawing maneuvers disappear. When you're done with that, round off all the corners so they're perfectly smooth. Yes, sanding takes time, but this is the soul of the project. Now you can really get into honing the board. When you ride this hot rod and see how sweet it is, you'll really thank yourself for putting in the time on this step. It's Zen time. Sand, grasshopper, sand. See image **j**.

31 Man . . . looks sweet, huh? Good job. Now it's time to let your drawing skills shine. With the thick felt-tip pen, draw something cool on the topside of the board. I like a nice rolling wave, myself. Whatever it is, sketch it out and draw it on some scrap wood first for practice. Once it looks the way you want, draw it on your deck. See image **k**.

32 Okay, now it's time to install the trucks, wheels, and bearings. Use the 1½-inch mounting hardware and ⅜-inch socket wrench to secure the trucks. The bolt heads should sink nicely into your predrilled holes. To install the wheels, press a bearing into each side with the ½-inch socket wrench. There should be two washers on the end of each axle. Make sure you place one on either side of each wheel when you mount them. After mounting each wheel, tighten each axle nut down tight. This will seat the bearings. Then back off each axle nut until the wheels spin freely but don't move side to side. See image **l**.

33 Cover the top of the deck with clear grip tape. Make sure the surface is clean, and slowly peel and stick the grip tape as you go. Make sure you don't create any bubbles. You should have extra tape hanging off the sides.

34 With the screwdriver held at a 45° angle, rub really hard along all the edges of the board. This will define a line at the edge so you can easily take the utility knife and cut off the excess grip tape. To do this, hold the grip tape level, but angle your utility knife in toward the middle of the board as you cut. Using this method, cut all the way around the edge of the board until all the excess is gone. See images **m** and **n**.

35 Carry the ⁹⁄₁₆-inch socket wrench with you as you take a few cruiser runs. Use the wrench to adjust the trucks to your liking. You don't want speed wobbles when you're bombing down the steepest hill in the neighborhood. If your trucks are way too loose, tighten those babies up, and vice versa. Have fun, and don't forget to let your kids borrow this board every once in a while!

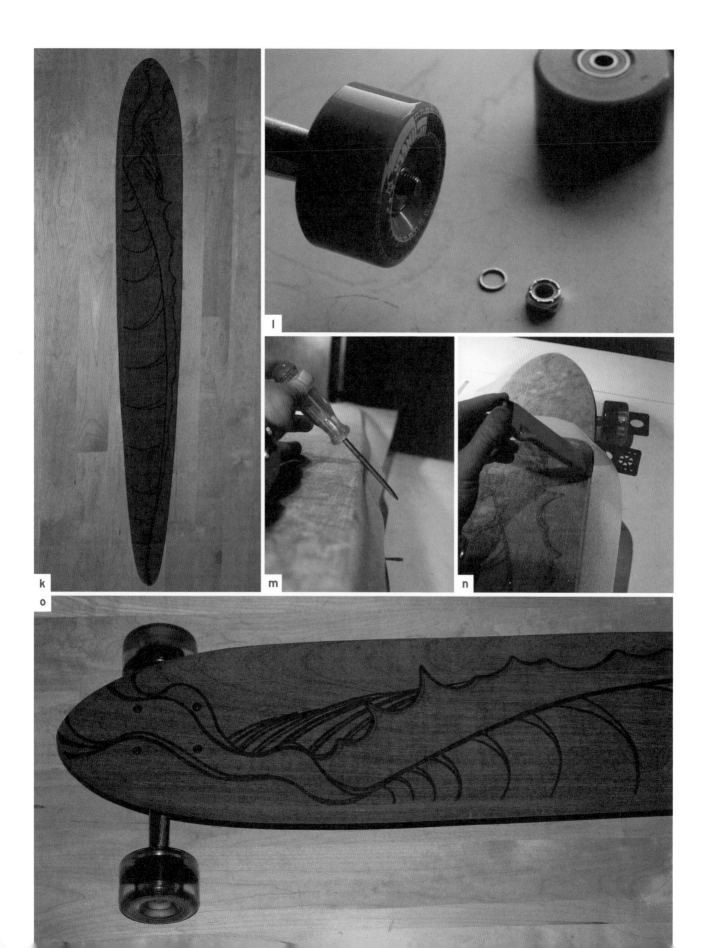

k

l

m

n

o

DOLLHOUSE

To a little girl, what's better than dolls? Not much, except for a house to put them in. A dollhouse doesn't, however, just provide a home for dolls; it provides a home for a girl's imagination. Here she can bring to life relationships and stories, acted out in her own little version of home sweet home. This is a challenging project, but I'm willing to bet that every hour you put into building it will bring her many, many more hours of playtime joy.

DIFFICULTY LEVEL:
Challenging

TIME INVOLVED:
A weekend

MATERIALS:

½-inch birch, cedar, or Douglas fir plywood, free of knots if possible (one 4-×-8-foot sheet, cut into four equal 2-×-4-foot pieces—you might be able to find these precut; if not, see if the store or lumberyard will cut them down to size for you)

Wallpaper (or any kind of paper with a fun, colorful print) for the interior (two 10-×-16-inch pieces, and three 10-×-10-inch pieces; optional)

2½-ounce tubes acrylic paint in the following colors: white (2 tubes); pink (2 tubes); red (1 tube); dark red, burgundy, or color of your choice for painting interior rooms (1 tube)

⅛-inch birch, cedar, or Douglas fir plywood
(one 2-×-6-foot sheet)

Forty or so stickers in girl-approved theme: flowers, butterflies, etc.

FASTENERS:

Wood glue

1¼-inch finishing nails (100-count box)

Rubber cement (optional)

TOOLS:

Hammer

Table saw

Drill with ¼-inch bit

Jigsaw with multipurpose blade

Electric sander with 60-grit sandpaper

2-inch-wide paintbrush

Chop saw

① From the ½-inch plywood, cut three equal-size pieces measuring 10 × 23 inches.

② Cut two more pieces of ½-inch plywood measuring 10 × 20 inches each.

③ Now sandwich two of the longer pieces, on their edges, in between the two shorter pieces to form a 10-×-20-×-24-inch box. Save the extra longer piece for the next step. Glue all edge joints with wood glue and attach with finishing nails spaced about 4 inches apart.

④ Place the remaining plywood piece in the middle of the box you've just made to divide the space into two floors, each measuring 10 × 9¼ × 23 inches. Again, apply wood glue to the edge joints and attach with finishing nails.

⑤ Using the table saw, cut a 45° bevel along the top edge of the sidewalls. See image **a**.

⑥ From the ½-inch plywood, cut three equal pieces measuring 10 × 9¼ inches. These will be the inner walls.

⑦ Now let's cut some 2½-×-7-inch doors out of the inner walls. Lay out the doors so they're 2 inches from the 9¼-inch edge. See image **b**. To cut out the top part of the door, drill a ¼-inch hole in one of the corners and use it as a starting point for the jigsaw. When you're done, set the inner walls aside until Step 18.

⑧ Okay, on to the roof. For that we'll need a couple more pieces of ½-inch plywood. Cut one piece to 12 × 20½ inches and the other to 12 × 20 inches. Miter one of the 12-inch edges on each board to a 45° angle.

⑨ Connect the two roof pieces at their non-mitered edges. Make sure the edge of the shorter piece is touching the face of the longer one and that mitered edges are facing down, not out. The roof should have a 45° pitch and two equal-length sides. Glue the edge joint and attach with finishing nails. See image **c**.

⑩ Now let's move on to the front wall of the house. We'll make it out of one of the 2-×-4-foot pieces of ½-inch plywood you've cut. Start by lightly drawing a centerline down its length with the pencil. Lay the 10-×-20-×-24-inch box you've built on top of the plywood so the outer and bottom edges of the box are all flush with the plywood sheet. Lay the roof into position onto the mitered edges of the box. Make sure the peak of the roof is lined up with the centerline on the ply. Now trace the inside edge of the roof onto the plywood with the pencil. See image **d**. The goal is to eventually have the roof rest on top of the front wall. Also trace a line under the eaves of the roof where they meet the outside edge of the box. This line should be 3½ inches from the bottom edge of the inside of the roof.

⑪ Using the table saw, cut the plywood sheet to the marks you just made. You should now have a piece of ply with three factory-cut edges, the bottom of which measures 24 inches and the sides of which measure approximately 19¾ inches. The top should have a 45° corner for the roof.

⑫ On the front wall piece, you are now going to measure and cut out a front door and windows. See **Dollhouse Facade**. The door should measure 4 × 7 inches centered, and ½ inch up from the bottom edge. Leaving ½ inch at the bottom will ensure that the door lines up with the floor later. To cut it out, drill ¼-inch holes in opposite corners of the door and saw from the hole to corner with the jigsaw. See image **e**.

⑬ Using that same technique, let's make some windows. They should measure 2½ × 4 inches, be 2½ inches from

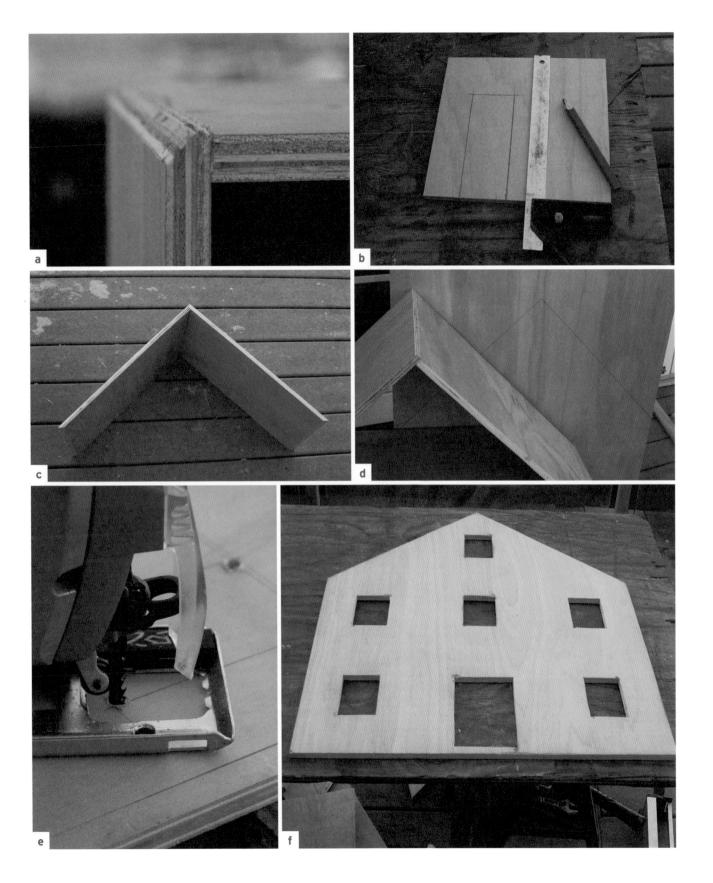

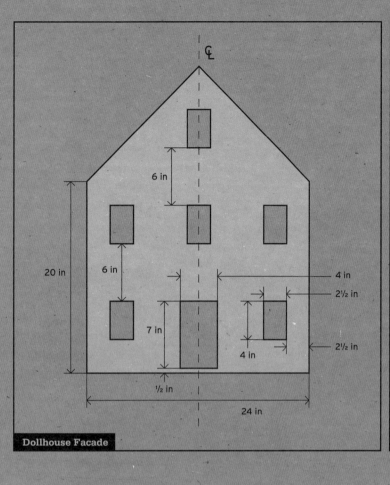

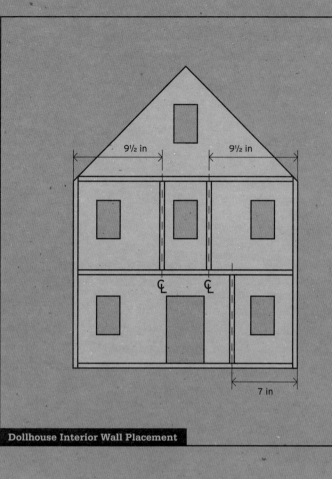

the outside edge of the plywood, and be flush with the top edge of the door.

14 Cut the second-story windows so that they are 6 inches above the ones on the first floor. Line the middle window up, on center, flush with the other two.

15 Cut the attic window on center, 6 inches above the middle second-story window. The front wall should now look like image **f**.

16 Sand all of the edges of the wood you've cut, especially the insides of the doors and windows.

17 If you want to add wallpaper to any of the rooms, now is the time. Just cut the paper to size using the walls as templates. To apply the wallpaper, coat both the paper and the wall with rubber cement, allow them to dry for about 30 minutes, and then press the cemented surfaces together. Be sure to line the paper up carefully—the rubber cement will tack right away. See image **g**. (Don't worry about the wallpaper for the inside of the front wall just yet. I'll explain how to do this in Step 19.)

18 Now let's install the three inner walls of the house. Place the first-floor wall 7 inches on center from the right-hand edge of the house. Place the second-story walls 9½ inches on center from the edges (measuring from the outside wall). Again, glue and nail the walls in place. See **Dollhouse Interior Wall Placement**.

19 To attach the front wall, start by laying the rest of the house (not including the roof) onto the inside of the front wall and ensuring all the edges are flush. Now trace along the inner walls to mark their positions onto the

inside of the front wall. These pencil lines will show you where to put the glue. Now slide the front wall out from underneath and lay it on the other side of the house with the pencil marks you just made facing out. Make sure the pencil marks are lying right over the walls they represent, and then flip the two pieces over. Now trace the inner walls again on this side of the front wall piece. These marks will tell you where to put the finishing nails. The lines on the inside of the front wall also give you the exact location for all the interior walls and floors so you can wallpaper it if you'd like. Simply overlap the wallpaper a little bit into the ½-inch sections between rooms/floors and rubber-cement the paper to the wood. Then glue all the edges, line up the front wall so it's flush, and nail it in place. Looking through the back of the house now, it should look like image **h**.

20 Line up the roof so that the marks you made on the underside line up with the mitered edges on the top of the house. Also make sure that the roof is flush against the back of the house. It should overhang the front of the house by 1½ inches. Mark this 1½-inch line on the underside of the roof. See image **i**.

21 Now paint the outside of the roof white. On the under-side, paint to the 1½-inch line (where the roof meets the front of the house) and 3½-inch lines (where the roof meets the side of the house under the eaves). If you go over a little, don't worry. It'll be covered up by the top edges of the house.

22 Okay, time for the trim work. See **Dollhouse Trim Pieces**. For the horizontal parts of the window trim, use

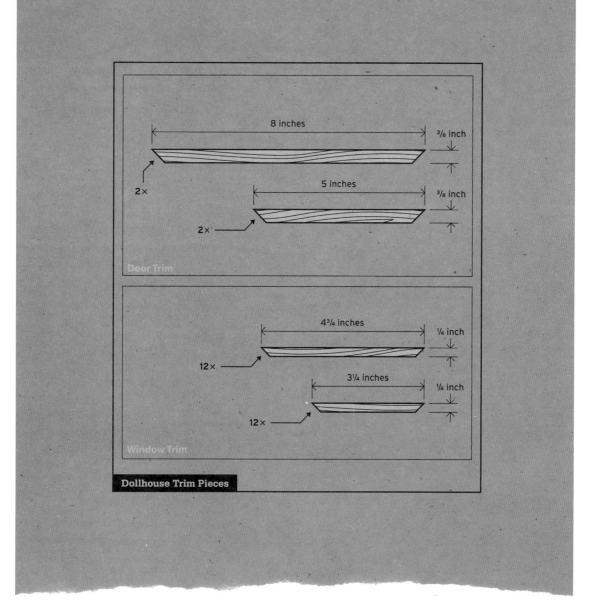

8 inches

³⁄₈ inch

2×

5 inches

³⁄₈ inch

2×

Door Trim

4³⁄₄ inches

¹⁄₄ inch

12×

3¹⁄₄ inches

¹⁄₄ inch

12×

Window Trim

Dollhouse Trim Pieces

the chop saw to cut the ⅛-inch plywood into three 2-foot-long strips ¼ inch wide. For the door trim, cut a ⅜-inch strip 2 feet long.

23 Cut the ¼-inch-wide strip into twelve 3¼-inch pieces, each with 45° miters on both ends. (All these mitered ends should face inward like a picture frame.)

24 From the ⅛-inch plywood cut twelve more ¼-inch-wide pieces 4¾ inches long, each with 45° mitered corners on both ends. These will be the vertical window trim pieces.

25 From the ⅜-inch door trim strip, cut two 5-inch pieces and two 8-inch pieces, each with 45° mitered corners on both ends.

26 Paint all the trim pieces white.

27 Paint the outside of the house pink.

28 After everything is dry, attach the roof with wood glue and finishing nails.

29 Glue the trim around the doors and windows, as if framing a picture. See image j.

30 Add some stickers and hire a mini moving van. It's time to move in the family!

j

TREASURE CHEST

Back in the days when men roamed the seas on square-riggers and brigantines, they kept their belongings in wooden sea chests. These chests were considered almost as valuable as the treasure they stored. Our kids need a place to keep the things they hold dear, too. But a good second-hand treasure chest is hard to find. Well, here's your chance to make a real beauty. It's as regal as any treasure chest there ever was and will do a fine job of housing your children's precious wares as they chart their own journeys, whether by land or sea. For this project, look for lumber with knotty character, the more the better.

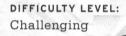

DIFFICULTY LEVEL:
Challenging

TIME INVOLVED:
A weekend

MATERIALS:

Two 6-foot 1×12 pine boards

One 6-foot 1×4 pine board

6 feet 1×2 embossed pine molding (pick a style that you like)

Gold or bronze paint

Fine-point gold metallic marker

Two 3½-inch brass chest handles

Eight 2-inch decorative brass corners

Two 2-inch decorative brass hinges

Old belt with interesting brass or gold buckle

Gold ship and/or sea-themed stickers (optional)

FASTENERS:

Wood glue

2-inch finishing nails (50-count box)

Brass upholstery nails (100 to allow for some being lost or bent)

TOOLS:

Chop saw

Hammer

Jigsaw with multipurpose blade

Electric sander with 60-grit sandpaper

2-inch paintbrush

Phillips-head screwdriver

INSTRUCTIONS:

1 It'll be easiest to start with the lid, so let's do that. From one of the 1×12 boards, cut a piece that's 22¼ inches long with the chop saw. (Keep in mind that a 1×12 piece of wood is actually ¾ × 11¼ inches.)

2 Now cut a 22¼-inch piece from the molding, giving both ends a 45° miter. Cut both miters as you would for a picture frame, so they point inward.

3 Cut another two pieces of molding to 11¼ inches. Cut 45° miters into one end of each piece, so you create right- and left-hand trim pieces for the lid that match the trim piece you made in the last step. See image **a**.

4 Glue all three pieces to the lid, ensuring they are flush with its outside edges and that the mitered corners fit snugly together. When complete, the open area on the underside of the lid will measure 20½ × 10½ inches. This area will cover the chest and allow room for hinges to be added along its back edge. See images **b** and **c**.

5 Now we're going to create the box part of the chest, starting with the floor. From the 1×12 piece, cut a piece measuring 9 × 18¾ inches.

6 Cut two more pieces for the shorter sides, each measuring 9 × 11¾ inches.

7 Now cut two pieces for the longer sides, each measuring 11¾ × 20¼ inches. When you're done, you should have five pieces of wood like those in image **d**.

8 Now let's attach the two shorter sides to the floor. Lay the floor piece on your workbench and apply wood glue to the two 9-inch sides. Make sure everything's snug and flush, and attach the sidewalls with finishing nails, as shown. See image **e**.

9 Now apply wood glue to the longer sides of the floor and along the vertical edges of the sidewalls. Lay the front and back walls of the chest in place. Again, make sure everything is snug and flush, and attach the walls with finishing nails, driving the nails into both the floor and the sidewalls. See image **f**.

10 Great. Let's move on to the base. From the 1×4 piece, cut two pieces each measuring 21¾ inches long.

11 From the same 1×4 piece, cut two more pieces measuring 10½ inches. Now you have four baseboards.

12 On one of the longer baseboards, draw a decorative arch. Measure in 2 inches to start the arch and finish 2 inches from the other end. Make it symmetrical. This piece will get cut out to form part of the base's legs. See image **g**. One easy way to make a symmetrical arch is to draw half of it onto a piece of foam core or mat board that's the same height as the base. Cut it out and you'll have a pattern. If you draw a centerline on the base, you can line your pattern up on either side of it and trace two perfect edges.

13 Draw a similar pattern (scaled for width) onto one of the short baseboards. This time, start 1½ inches in and finish the same distance from the other end.

14 Cut out the long and short patterned pieces with a jigsaw and use each piece as a template for transferring the pattern to the other long and short baseboards. Cut out the remaining pieces. See image **h**.

15 Set the box on its end and prepare to attach the short baseboard. The baseboard should overlap the box by 1½ inches. Mark this position on the box. Apply wood glue within your marks and set the piece in place. Attach with 2-inch finishing nails, being careful to drive the nails through the sidewalls into the edge of the floor, not into the interior of the box itself.

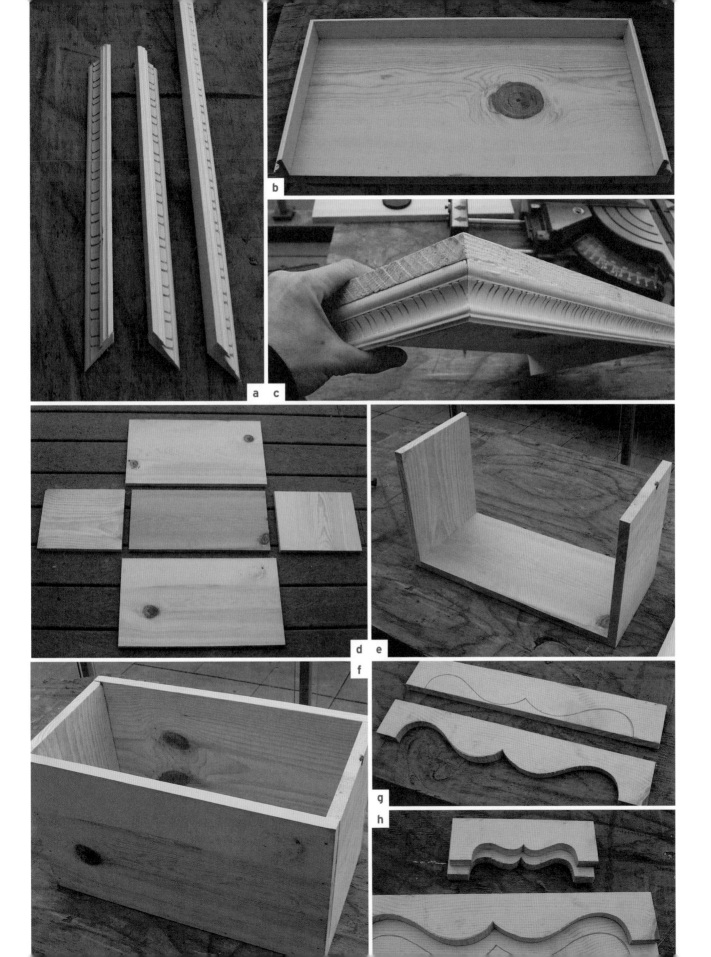

16 Attach the remaining base pieces in the same way, using the same 1½-inch overlap. See image **i**.

17 Sand the outside of the box and wipe off the dust.

18 Paint the entire box with the gold or bronze paint, starting with the trim. Do the insides and bottom as well. Once you've painted the entire chest, the trim should be dry enough to decorate with the marker. Trace the grooves in the trim that you'd like to highlight, then fill in those portions with your metallic marker.

19 Lay the hinges over the top edge of the chest's back wall. They should be 4 inches from the corners and fold 90° over the edge of the wall. See image **j**. Screw the hinges in place.

20 Lay the chest on its back, resting the hinges on the inside of the lid. Attach one screw per hinge at first, then open and close the lid a few times. If it fits smoothly and doesn't rub anywhere, attach the final screws to secure it in place. If the lid does rub and you haven't made any building mistakes, pull out the screws, separate the box and lid slightly, and again attach each hinge with one screw, this time using a different hole. When everything fits, drive in the final screws. See image **k**.

21 Attach the brass handles to the sides of the chest, 9 inches on center from the ground up. Make sure there's enough room to close the lid if you alter their placement at all.

22 Add the decorative corners to the four corners on the top of the lid and the four corners on the bottom of the base. Overtighten the screws on the bottom of the base so the chest rests on the brass corner pieces, not on the heads of the screws themselves. See image **l**.

23 Now we're going to attach the belt using the brass upholstery nails. Lay the box on its back again (the side with the hinges) and position the belt so the buckle is at about the same height as the handles on the sides of the chest. When you've got it where you want it, pull the belt taut and mark it where it crosses the top edge of the base. Cut the belt along that mark and nail it, on

center, to the front of the chest using six of the brass nails. See image **m**.

24 Put the chest back on its feet and thread the cut-off portion of the belt (the end with holes in it) into the buckle. Lay the loose end over the top of the lid and down the back of the chest. This piece of the belt will be the strap that keeps the lid closed. Adjust the length of belt that passes through the buckle on the front side so the buckle is positioned where you like it, leaving enough room for it to reach the top of the baseboard on the back of the chest. Pull the loose end of the belt taut across the top of the chest and down across the back; mark where it lines up with the top edge of the baseboard. Cut the strap to your mark and secure it to the back of the chest with six brass nails, two near the bottom edge, two in the middle, and two near the top. Secure it to the lid with brass nails, too, but don't nail it to the front of the chest.

25 Now for some finishing touches. To start, we'll tack a row of brass upholstery nails vertically up either side of the outside edges of the chest's walls. Place the first nail 1 inch above the baseboard and ¾ inch in from the edge. Continue to space nails 1 inch apart and ¾ inch in from the edge—eight nails will fit perfectly and allow enough room for the lid to close without hitting any of the nails. See images **n** and **o**. You'll do two rows per edge, eight rows total. This will give the appearance that they are holding the chest together and add to the overall seafaring look of the piece. See image **p**.

26 Apply stickers or other ornamental items to enhance the look of the chest, personalizing it to your satisfaction. Ah, there you go, lad! Your treasure chest is complete!

If the recipient of this treasure chest plans on burying it once it's filled with loot, make sure he or she draws a map first. Don't let it fall into the wrong hands! Other privateers, swashbucklers, hucksters, and little brothers and sisters come to mind. On second thought, it'd be a shame to bury a gem like this. I advise drawing up a phony treasure map instead, like real pirates used to do. That'll keep it safe and keep any would-be plunderers guessing! Yo-ho-ho!

BIKE JUMP

Let me guess—your kids have learned how to ride bikes and now they want to start their BMX careers by jumping them over stuff? I know what they're thinking, too: cinder blocks and a piece of plywood, right? Well, that might work the first few times, but after a couple good launches, the wood will start to split. Then they'll be in danger of cracking through the ramp in a Napoleon Dynamite–style endo. To make sure your kids' thrill seeking doesn't send you hospital seeking, build them a solid set of jumps (and invest in some helmets and pads). Not only are they totally sweet, they have some nice extra features. Once the young ones master these, they'll be on to the X Games in no time.

DIFFICULTY LEVEL:
Challenging

TIME INVOLVED:
A weekend

MATERIALS:

Five 8-foot 2×4 Douglas fir boards

One 4-foot 1×4 pine board

¾-inch plywood subflooring (one 4-×-8-foot sheet, cut into four equal 2-×-4-foot pieces)

½-inch plywood (one 4-×-8-foot sheet, cut into four equal 2-×-4-foot pieces)*

Four 3-inch light-duty, non-swiveling caster wheels

Four 2-foot concrete stakes

Eight ½-inch pipe clamps

Have the lumberyard cut the ½-inch plywood horizontally, i.e., so that the grain will run across the resulting 2-×-4-foot sheet perpendicularly from long edge to long edge. Cutting it this way will make it possible for the plywood to conform to the curve of the ramps.

FASTENERS:

3-inch wood screws (100-count box)

2-inch wood screws (100-count box)

TOOLS:

Carpenter's square

Circular saw

Drill with Phillips-head and ⅛-inch bits

1 Cut all the 2×4 pieces and 1×4 pieces into 22½-inch-long pieces. The 2×4 pieces will be crossbars, and the 1×4 pieces will be front-edge pieces. You should have twenty of the 2×4 pieces and two of the 1×4 pieces when you're done. We'll be making two ramps. You can make them simultaneously or one after the other, whichever you prefer.

2 Lay one of the ¾-inch plywood sheets on your work surface. We'll be making a series of marks on it to define the curve of the ramp. I'll guide you through it. Have a look at the **Bike Jump Sidewall** illustration, which will make it easier to follow.

3 Make the first mark 6 inches from both the top and right-hand edges. From this mark, use the carpenter's square to draw a straight horizontal line to the right-hand edge. When marking the ply, use a good-sized cross or an X. You'll need to see your marks after you cut out the curve.

4 Make a mark at the lower left edge, 1 inch from the bottom of the same sheet.

5 Make a mark 12 inches down from the top edge and 16½ inches from the right-hand edge.

6 Make a mark 16 inches down from the top edge and 25½ inches from the right-hand edge.

7 Make a mark 18 inches down from the top edge and 30¾ inches from the right-hand edge.

8 Make a mark 20 inches down from the top edge and 36¾ inches from the right-hand edge.

9 Great. Now starting from the upper right-hand mark, draw a smooth, continuous freehand curve down to the mark in the lower left-hand corner.

10 Using your circular saw, cut along the curve. Also cut along the straight 6-inch line in the top-right corner. This will form one side of the ramp.

11 Using the piece you just made as a template, and the remaining ¾-inch plywood, make three more identical pieces.

12 Now we're going to mark the spots along the curve where the 2×4 pieces will go. Grab a 2×4 piece (a short cut-off piece will do) and the first sidewall that you made. Place the end of the 2×4 piece onto the sidewall at what will be the start of the ramp so that its wider edge is flush with the curve of the ramp and its bottom corner touches the bottom edge of the sidewall. See image **a**. Now trace the three edges of the 2×4 piece onto the sidewall. (The fourth edge is flush to the curve, so you can't trace that one.)

13 Move the 2×4 piece so it's flush against the outline that you made in the last step and trace. Again, the 2×4 piece should be flush with the curve of the sidewall as well. See image **b**.

14 Let's trace a few more. Move the 2×4 piece so it is still flush with the curve, and draw an outline when its left-hand corner is on the following marks you made earlier: 12 inches, 16 inches, 18 inches, and 20 inches. Draw one more outline with the right-hand corner of the 2×4 piece placed where the curve meets the 6-inch horizontal line in the upper right-hand part of the sidewall.

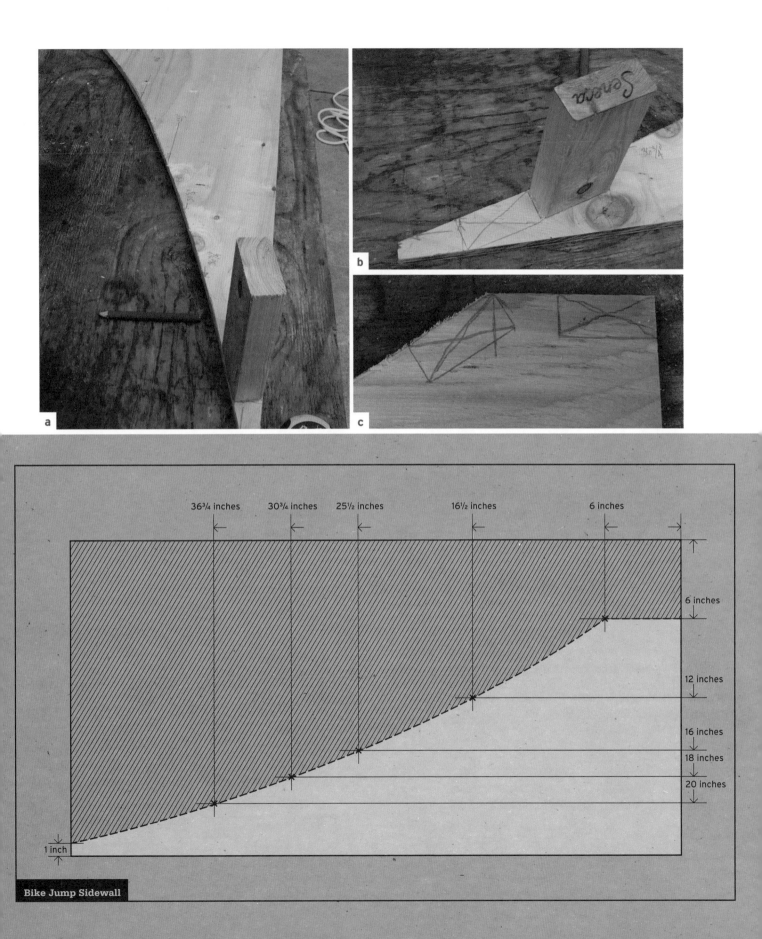

36¾ inches   30¾ inches   25½ inches   16½ inches   6 inches

6 inches

12 inches

16 inches

18 inches

20 inches

1 inch

Bike Jump Sidewall

15 Draw another outline with the 2×4 piece in the topmost right-hand corner of the ramp. See image **c**.

16 Draw one more 2×4 outline in the lower right-hand corner, with the wide side flush with the lower edge of the sidewall. Draw a final outline along the lower edge 12 inches from the one you just made. Repeat Steps 2 to 16 on another piece of ¾-inch plywood for the second jump.

17 Now let's attach 10 of the 2×4 crossbars to the sidewall using our outlines as a guide. They'll go on the other side of the sidewall, not on the side where we made our marks. (Seeing the outlines will help you know where to drive the screws.) Be sure to take extra care to ensure the boards are flush with the edge of the sidewall. To attach them, use three 3-inch wood screws for each end of each 2×4 piece, using the outlines as a guide for where to place the screws. See images **d** and **e**. You may find that

things go a little faster if you get all of the screws started, then line up the boards and drive them in.

18 Once that's done, flip the ramp over onto its side. Are the crossbars pointing up? Good. Now connect them to the other piece of plywood as in the last step. Start by lining up and attaching the crossbars at the corners and at the front of the ramp, then move on to the ones along the curve. See images **f** and **g**.

19 Now place one of the 1×4 pieces between the two sidewalls at the start of the ramp, in front of the first 2×4 piece. It should be flush with both edges of the sidewalls and the top of the 2×4 piece. It will stick out past the front of the ramp sidewalls by an inch or so. Predrill two holes through the ramp into either side of the 1×4 piece and attach using 3-inch wood screws. See image **h**.

20 Now let's attach one of the pieces of ½-inch plywood to the curve of our ramp. Position the plywood so it is flush with the sides of the ramp but overhangs the front of it by 4 inches. See image **i**.

21 You'll attach the plywood to the ramp by screwing it into each of the 2×4 crossbars, using four 2-inch wood screws per crossbar. Start at the front edge of the ramp and work your way up, placing the four screws in the same evenly spaced pattern on each crossbar. (Measure and make a note of where you're placing the screws. We want to know where they are because we'll need to avoid them when we add the second layer of plywood later on.) The end of the plywood will be 2 inches from the top of the ramp. See how having the grain perpendicular to the sides of the ramp helps the plywood bend?

22 Grab another piece of the ½-inch plywood. This will be our ramp's top layer. Before we use it though, cut 2 inches off of the 2-foot end. Using four 2-inch wood screws, add this cut-off piece to the top of the ramp, filling in the gap left by the first piece of plywood.

23 Now, from the leftover ¾-inch plywood, cut a piece measuring 2 × 6 inches. Lay this on the top, flat part of the ramp so it's flush with the sides and butts up against the little filler piece from the last step. When it's lined up, screw it down with six 2-inch wood screws. Drive three screws into the crossbar at the back of the ramp, one toward each edge, and one in the middle. Drive the other screws in close to the front edge of the plywood (about ½ inch from the edge). These screws will bite into the side of the crossbar at the top of the curve of the ramp.

24 Grab the plywood that you cut in Step 22 and butt its short side up against the ¾-inch ply at the top of the ramp. Using four 2-inch wood screws per crossbar, attach the plywood to the ramp, starting at the top edge this time. Work your way down, avoiding the screws holding down the first layer of plywood. When you've done that, you'll be 4 inches shy of the bottom. Don't worry, though. This difference in heights won't be noticeable when the ramp is in use. See images **j** and **k**.

25 Using 2-inch wood screws, attach the casters to the right sidewall of the ramp, placing them along the back edge, at the top and bottom. Make sure to drive the screws through the sidewall and into the 2×4 pieces behind it.

26 Place one concrete stake vertically along each side of the ramp near the top where it transitions from curve to flat. Attach a pair of pipe clamps to the sidewall using 2-inch wood screws. (Try to go into the 2×4 pieces behind the sidewall.) Place one clamp at the top and one at the bottom. See image **l**. Do the same for the other side. When the ramps are being used on a lawn, drive the stakes into the ground until they're flush with the top. (To remove them, just lift up one side of the ramp and they'll wiggle loose.) Take the stakes out when you're not using them so no one accidentally hits one.

27 Did you make two ramps simultaneously? If so, you're done. If not, make another one just like the first one—your aspiring BMXers will need a place to land.

28 Place the jumps about 6 feet apart and let your budding BMXers air 'em out. As your BMX stars get better, pull the ramps farther apart. Have them add a trick or two for style points!

l

ZIP LINE

For that *Mission Impossible* feeling, nothing beats a zip line. Just site an unobstructed, 50-foot path between two fixed objects with a little gravity on their side, and you're in business. Suspend the line over some difficult-to-access (but not neck-breaking) terrain and your kids will have the makings for some serious, elevation-assisted thrills.

DIFFICULTY LEVEL:
Challenging

TIME INVOLVED:
A weekend

MATERIALS:

6 feet garden hose or plastic drip line

50 feet ⅜- to ½-inch stainless steel cable

2-foot 2×8 redwood board

6 to 8 feet ½-inch braided-nylon sailing or mountaineering rope

Double-wheeled pulley (or single-wheel, if your kids want to spin while they zip)

¼-inch braided nylon rope (enough to go from the bottom of the cable to within 5 feet of the ground)

FASTENERS:

¾-inch wire rope clips (6)

3-inch wood screws (6)

1-inch threaded D-shackle

TOOLS:

Duct tape

Drill with Phillips-head and ¾-inch bit

Socket wrench with socket to fit wire rope clips

Cable cutters or electric saw with metal-cutting blade

NOTE: For details on tying the knots referred to in this project, refer to the Knots section on page 162.

Note: If you don't have two suitable trees and want to make your own substitute, see Step 12. It's not ideal—I recommend you use trees. This method will take a lot of sweat, but, if you have to have a zip line, this is an option. You will need the following additional materials and tools for the one end of the zip line without a tree.

MATERIALS:

14-foot 4×6 pressure-treated beam

Cement, fencepost mix (fourteen 80-pound bags)

FASTENERS:

(Don't skimp on hardware—the sizes specified here can handle loads of more than 2,000 pounds.)

½-inch nut and washer (1 each)

Stakes, for staking down the beam (4)

½-inch quick link

Wire-rope thimble to fit your cable dimension

Forged eyebolt (1-inch diameter hole, ½-×-8-inch shaft)

TOOLS:

Socket wrench with ½-inch socket

Shovel

Auger with ⅝-inch bit

Electric sander with a few sheets of 60-grit sandpaper

1 Find two solid, level, fixed points approximately 50 to 200 feet apart—for example, a high and a low point in two trees, a tree and a building, or two buildings. Ultimately, the line should have about 4° of slope to it. Don't make it too steep. If you're going to use a building, make sure you're okay with drilling a ¼-inch hole in one of the vertical support beams.

2 Walk along the path of the proposed zip line and clear any branches that might snag riders on their way down. If the launch point is in a tree, climb up and do the same there.

3 Cut the garden hose into two 3-foot pieces. Duct-tape the ends of the cable and pass one end through one of the pieces of hose.

4 Secure the stainless-steel cable around the "launch tree," making sure that only the hose, and not the cable, touches the tree. The wire rope clips will attach the end of the cable to itself. Using a socket wrench, place the clips so they're spaced 6 inches apart, with the first one 6 inches from the tree. See image **a**. If possible, wrap the cable over a branch as you pass it around the tree to keep it from sagging. If there aren't any branches in sight, drive a 3-inch wood screw into the back of the tree, leaving 1 inch exposed. If you rest the cable/hose on the screw, it will prevent any sag.

5 Okay, now let's build the seat that you'll attach to the zip-line pulley. Cut the redwood board in half so you end up with two equal pieces.

6 Screw the pieces together using four 3-inch wood screws, one near each corner of the seat. Drive the screws in at a slight angle toward the middle so they don't poke out the other side.

7 Drill a ¾-inch hole in the center of the two boards and heavily sand all the sides and edges, including the hole you just drilled, until everything is very smooth.

8 Stick one end of the ½-inch rope through the center hole and tie a stopper knot leaving about 12 inches of excess rope under the seat.

9 Grab the remaining rope coming out through the top of the seat and tie it to the D-shackle. Let's use a bowline for that. When tying the bowline, take an extra turn around the D-shackle. This will reduce chafing. See image **b**. Don't attach it to the pulley yet, though.

10 Now find the loose end of the cable and pass it through the pulley and the other 3-foot section of garden hose.

11 Take the cable to the other fixed point and attach it as you did on the launch tree, ensuring that the cable is very tight before you cinch it with the wire rope clips, again spaced 6 inches apart, with the first one 6 inches from the tree. If the cable is too long after you've attached the wire rope clips, cut it with the cable cutter.

12 This is an optional step. If one or both of the fixed points is one you need to build yourself, this is how you do it:

a. Auger a ⅝-inch hole through one of the beams about 5 inches from the end. Put the hole into the narrower side of the beam. Insert the forged eyebolt into the hole and attach the washer and nut using the socket wrench with the ½-inch socket. See **Attaching the Eyebolt to the Post**.

b. Using the shovel, dig a hole 30 inches wide and 5 feet deep.

c. Center the beam in the hole with the eyebolt end up, and the eyebolt facing the other zip line anchor point.

d. Stake down the beam to ensure it will stay vertically level when you pour the cement. Now mix the cement and pour it in the hole. Make sure to follow the directions on the bag for set time. Don't put tension on the line before the cement has fully set.

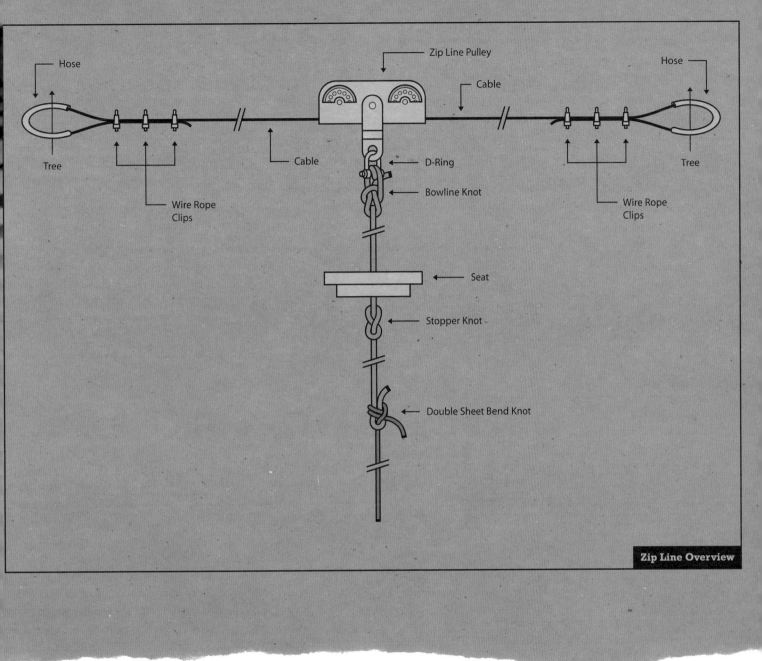

Hose

Tree

Wire Rope
Clips

Cable

Zip Line Pulley

Cable

D-Ring

Bowline Knot

Seat

Stopper Knot

Double Sheet Bend Knot

Hose

Tree

Wire Rope
Clips

e. Once the concrete has set, attach and tighten the zip line, but use a quick link and a wire rope thimble instead of a piece of gardening hose when attaching the eyebolt. The wire rope thimble will fit perfectly into the bight of the wire rope and keep it from forming too small of an angle against the quick link. Make sure the quick link is right up against the wire rope thimble. See image **c**.

13 Now that the line is taught, attach the seat assembly to the pulley using the D-shackle. Check the zip line over to make sure everything's working and double-check that the flight path is clear of any potential snags. Okay? Then it's time for a test run. Pull the seat up to the launch point and let it go. It should travel very slowly to the other side. Don't worry—it'll go a lot faster when there's weight on it.

14 Okay, let's do a little quality-control check. Position a person at either end of the line and take the seat and pulley to the middle of the run. Put a little weight on it. Is everything cool? Put a little more weight on the seat. Check with your spotters at the ends of the line. Is anything moving or slipping? No? Okay, then sit on the seat. Is everything still buttoned up? Great. Bounce around on the seat. If everything is still solid, you're ready to send a live test pilot for the zip's maiden run.

15 If your test pilot is going too fast for a reasonable landing, lower the cable on the takeoff end and try again. When you have the angle of flight dialed in, screw a 3-inch wood screw into the back of the tree just below the cable/hose to prevent the angle from changing. Leave ½ inch sticking out, so the cable doesn't slide down. You may also need to raise or lower the height of the line for lighter or heavier kids. Add a 3-inch wood screw for each different cable position.

16 As a final touch, use a single (or double, for extra security) sheet bend to tie the ¼-inch rope to the tail end of the line under the seat. This will help zip-line riders retrieve the seat and pull it back up the launch area.

17 Zips ahoy!

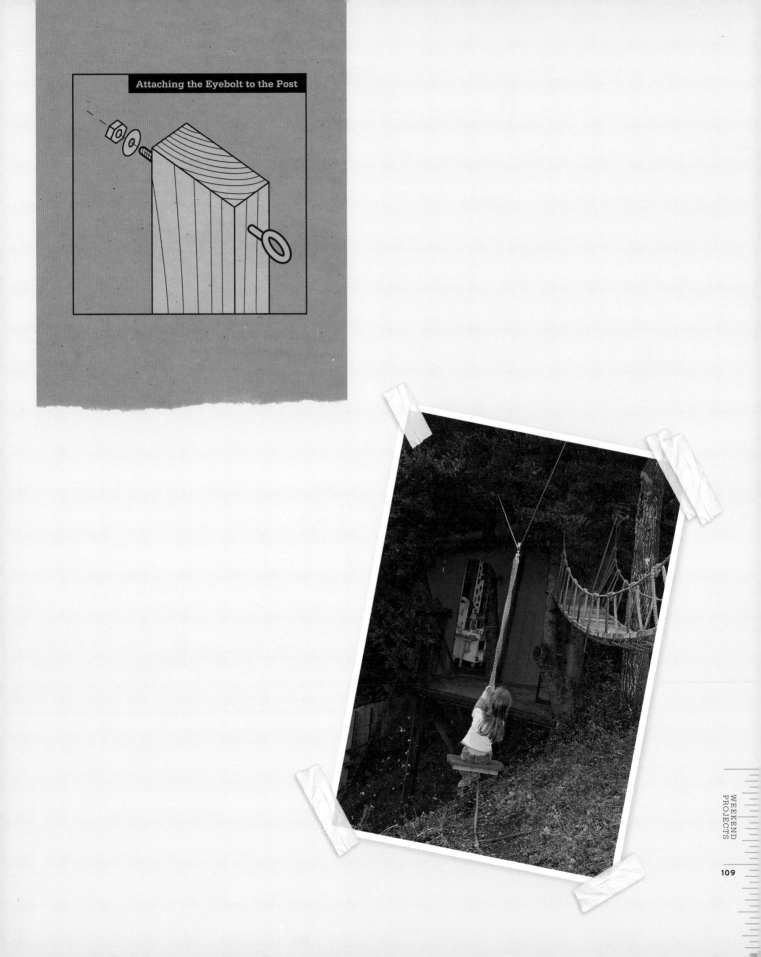

Attaching the Eyebolt to the Post

TREE HOUSE

I bet your kids wish they had their own place. Oh, what's that? They're not even 12 and too young to move out? Maybe just a crash pad, then—a place to get away from it all . . . and to chuck water balloons from! The key thing, of course, is location, location, location. I'd recommend the crook of a good, solid tree. It's prime real estate! And they'll already be familiar with the neighborhood. I tell ya, they'll love the views. Have them call their contractor right away. That's you, Handy Dad!

DIFFICULTY LEVEL:
Challenging

TIME INVOLVED:
A weekend

MATERIALS:

Two 8-foot 2×4 Douglas fir, redwood, or pressure-treated lumber boards

Twelve 10-foot 2×6 Douglas fir, redwood, or pressure-treated lumber boards

Two 4-×-8-foot sheets 1-inch plywood subflooring

Nine 10-foot 2×4 Douglas fir, redwood, or pressure-treated lumber boards

4-×-30-foot roll heavy-duty netting or construction mesh, preferably GeoTech

FASTENERS:

3-inch wood screws (200-count box)

½-×-6-inch lag bolts with washers (6 each)

TOOLS:

Drill with Phillips-head and ¼-inch bit

Circular saw

Heavy-duty stapler and ⅜-inch staples

Socket wrench with ½-inch socket

INSTRUCTIONS:

1 First, put your building inspector—I mean, tree inspector—hat on. You're looking for a tree with three or more distinct branches that are at least 6 inches thick and all fan out from the same spot on the trunk.

2 Create a ladder up into the canopy with as many 12-inch pieces of 8-foot 2×4 timber as it takes to do the job. Position the rungs on the tree in 1-foot increments, and attach each rung with three 3-inch wood screws. Drive the screws into the center of the rung in a triangular pattern, spacing them far enough apart that the rung won't twist when you step on it with a heavy load, but not so far apart that the screw doesn't bite well because of the curvature of the tree.

3 Okay, let's attach one of the 2×6 pieces to two of the branches you've selected. The beam should be on the exterior side of the branches (farther from the trunk), and at such a height that the ends extend only about 6 inches past each branch. Temporarily attach the beam by driving one 3-inch wood screw into each branch. Make sure that the sides of the beam are perpendicular to the ground. If they're not, add shims until they are. Then predrill holes for the 6-inch lag bolt using the ¼-inch drill bit. Place the hole through the 2×6 piece at the spot where it comes in contact with the thickest part of the branch. Make sure each lag bolt has a washer and use the socket wrench to bury them into the tree as far as you can, permanently securing the board in place. (When I say "bury," I mean drive the bolt down into the beam until the top of it is flush with the beam's surface, since we'll have to attach another beam on top of this one later. Also, do your best to keep the sides of the board perpendicular to the ground.)

4 Attach two more 2×6 pieces to the tree as in the previous step, making sure the wide sides of the beams are perpendicular to the ground. If the ends of your beams overlap, mark the point where they cross, bring them back down to your work bench, and cut them with the

circular saw. At the end of this step you should have a triangular foundation. See **Shimming the Beams** and **Trimming the Beams**.

5 At this point, each of the three 2×6 beams should be attached to the tree in two places with 6-inch lag bolts and washers. Screw the ends of the boards to each other where they touch using three 3-inch wood screws. See image **a**.

6 Now, using more 2×6 pieces as joists, connect all the pieces of the foundation. Place them every 16 inches, parallel to one of the outside boards, and drive three 3-inch wood screws through the outside edge of the foundation to secure each one. See image **b**.

7 With a sheet of the 1-inch subflooring, cover as much of the foundation as you can. Attach it with 3-inch wood screws every 18 inches along each joist. Try to situate the subflooring so one edge of it lies exactly on the centerline of one of the joists. If this is difficult to do, add another joist under the edge of the subflooring. Cover the entire inside dimension of the foundation flush with the edge, leaving one square hole about 18 inches wide next to your kids' favorite branch so that they can access the fort from below, but don't leave a hole so big that they'll fall into it from above.

8 Now we'll add a railing 42 inches up from the foundation. We'll use the 10-foot 2×4 pieces and attach them to the same branches we used for the foundation. Again form a triangle, attaching each board to the branches using three 3-inch wood screws instead of lag bolts this time. Make sure the boards are level. Finish by screwing the corners together with three 3-inch wood screws per corner.

9 Now wrap the heavy-duty netting around both the railing and the foundation, pulling it very tight and stapling it every 2 inches, top and bottom. Drive the staples in at a 45° angle (leaning away from the pull of the netting) to give them more strength. Trim any excess. See image **c**.

10 Finish the structure off by attaching a 10-foot 2×4 piece to each outside edge of both the railing and the foundation, using 3-inch wood screws every 6 inches. Doing this will not only hold the netting in place, but also will strengthen the railing and foundation.

11 That's it! Invite your kids up so they can soak up the view from their top-floor tree loft. Be sure to have them thank their contractor for all his hard work!

Shimming the Beams

Place a piece of scrap 2×4 to shim the 2×6 so its sides are perpendicular to the ground.

Trimming the Beams

Lay boards on top of one another, mark, and cut.

STUNT DUMMY/ ABOMINABLE SNOWMAN

There are certain stunts that just shouldn't be attempted by mere mortals. For those stunts, you need a stand-in who can take a tumble without breaking a bone. Enter the Stunt Dummy/Abominable Snowman. He's life-sized, stuffed with cotton filling, and perfect for launching off cliffs or withstanding an epic ten-kid dog pile.

DIFFICULTY LEVEL:
Challenging (or super-challenging for the Abominable Snowman)

TIME INVOLVED:
A weekend

MATERIALS FOR STUNT DUMMY:

2 yards felt fabric in a dark color so the dirt doesn't show so much when he gets a face full of it

Two 1-inch buttons, for eyes

½-inch button, for nose

5 pounds Hollofil or cotton stuffing

MATERIALS FOR ABOMINABLE SNOWMAN:

2 yards 1½-inch-pile faux fur, white

¼ yard ¼-inch-pile faux fur, black for pads of hands and feet

¼ yard ¾-inch-pile faux fur, gray, for around face

¼ yard felt in gray (for claws, lips, and face), white (for eyes and teeth), and black (for eyes, nose, and mouth)

5 pounds Hollofil or cotton stuffing

FASTENERS:

Large safety pins (about 20)

Thread to match the color of your material (1 spool)

White thread, to sew mouth design (1 spool)

TOOLS:

Scissors

Sewing machine

Extra machine needles, just in case

Large black felt-tip pen, or chalk to mark felt fabric

Ruler

INSTRUCTIONS:

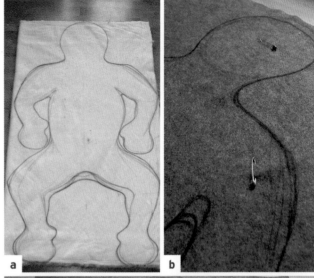

① Fold the felt (or faux fur) perfectly in half lengthwise. (If you're using fur, make sure the furry side is on the inside of the fold.)

② Have your child lie down on the fabric, feet slightly apart. Make sure your kid's head and feet fit on the fabric, and trace the outline of the body making your best police-style body outline on the fabric. Be sure to leave at least 1 inch of fabric around the outside edge of the outline all the way around. See image **a**.

③ Safety-pin the two pieces of felt together along the torso, the limbs, and the head, making sure to put the pins close to the *inside* edge of your outline. See images **b**, **c**, and **d**.

④ Using a good pair of scissors, cut around the body outline, staying 1 inch outside of it as you go. See images **e** and **f**.

⑤ If you are choosing to make the Abominable Snowman, sew paws with claws on the hands and feet of one of the pieces of fabric, on the furry side. On the furry side of the other piece, sew a face. The face and paws should be on opposite pieces of fabric so that the hands and feet end up on the underside of the body when it's all done. Now pin the two pieces of fabric together fur side to fur side (inside out). See images **g**, **h**, and **i**.

⑥ Use the sewing machine to sew the two pieces of felt (or faux fur) together, starting at one ear. Sew all the way around the body, ending at the other ear and leaving the top of the head open. The line you traced initially makes a useful guide as you sew. Just align it with the outside edge of the presser foot. Sew about ¾ inch away from the line, leaving ¼ inch of fabric on the edge. Be sure to double back on the stitching at the beginning and end to secure it. It would also be a good idea to double-stitch the armpits and crotch—these areas take a lot of abuse

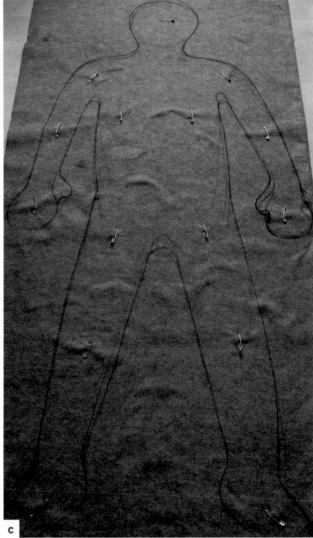

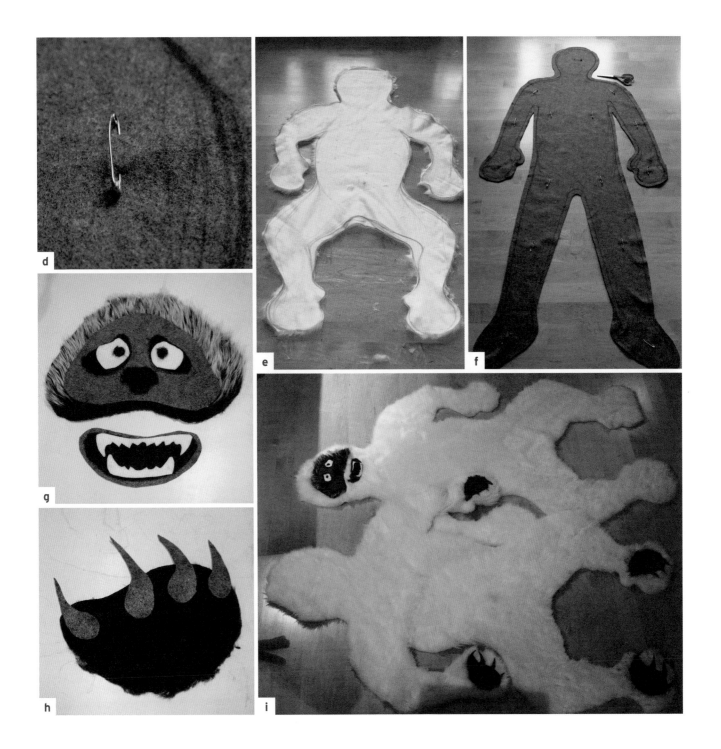

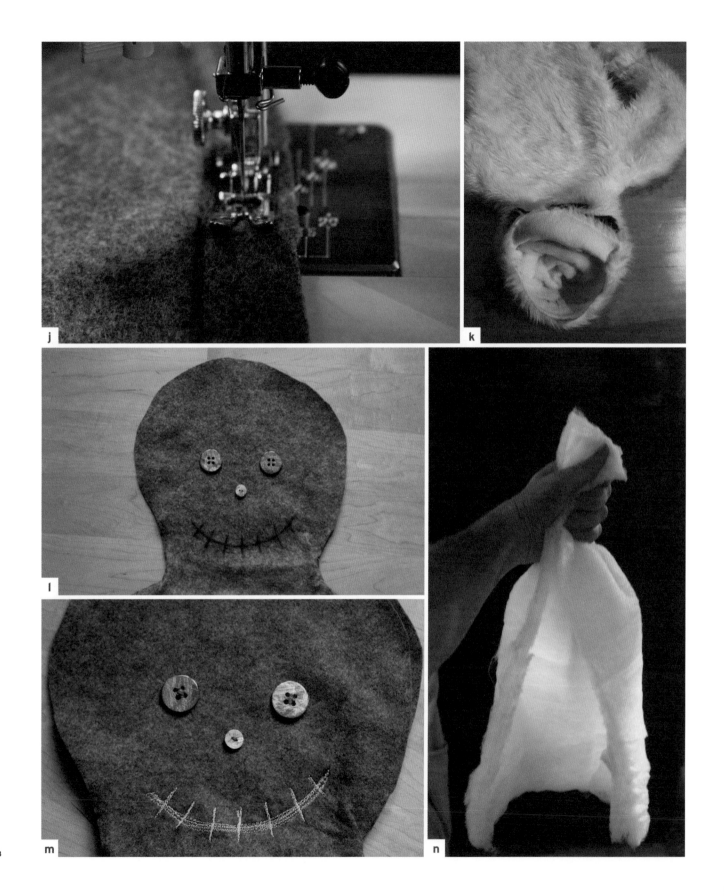

when fights break out over who gets to play with it when it's done, and during the normal abuse of stunt time. See image **j**.

7 Turn the entire body inside out (actually, it'll be right-side out once you do this). It should be completely sewn together except for an opening at the top of the head. See image **k**.

8 If you're making the Stunt Dummy, now is the time to sew the face on. Pick the side that will be the front and, using the darker thread, sew on the 1-inch eye buttons. Remember, this is your dummy, so you can make him (or her) look any way you want. The eyes can be sewn shut (much like the mouth in the next step) or just one can, so it looks like a wink. It's your call. Sew on the ½-inch nose button. Then draw on a huge smile with the pen or chalk, whichever shows up better. I chose a normal face, but feel free to improvise. See image **l**.

9 With the white thread, sew over the mouth line six or eight times to make it really visible. Now you can add seven vertical stitches (for good luck—he might need it) to make it look like his mouth is sewn shut. See image **m**.

10 Okay, he doesn't have any bones, but he'll still need guts (in more ways than one). Starting with 18-inch pieces of Hollofil (see image **n**), stuff the hands and feet first. The best way is to grab one end of the Hollofil and push it into the ends of the limbs. Use a ruler to push it into the small voids. Make a decision now whether you want this guy to be buff and tough or squeezably soft. The more you pump him full of Hollofil, the buffer he'll be. More fill means he'll be more fun to tackle and more lifelike for those long falls. Less means he'll be easier to chuck around.

11 Alright, doctor—time to stitch this patient up. Fill the head up with the desired amount of fill, then push the fill down into the neck a bit to give yourself room to sew the head shut. Fold both seams inward like the others, and stitch by hand—or use the sewing machine, if there's enough room. Once his melon is all laced up, push the fill back into the head.

12 To give this guy a little more definition, sew some creases in the joints. Just push the fill out of the way and sew in toward the limbs, perpendicular to the dummy's outside edge. This technique works for making thumbs and feet as well as elbows and knees. See image **o**.

13 Your dummy is ready for action. From now on, any brilliant, harebrained, or questionable scheme that your kids come up with that may potentially involve bodily injury can be tested by a largely indestructible stand-in. Your family health plan thanks you.

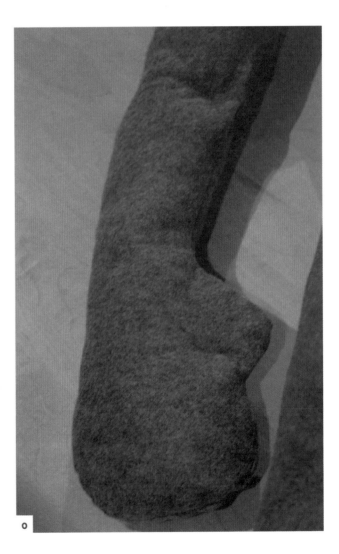

o

LIGHT BOX

A nightlight is okay, but what if instead you could build your kids a magic box with which they could see the surface of the ocean from ten leagues underwater, or see through the mist of a redwood forest? What if they could see into outer space or look down across the surface of the earth? What's that? No, it's not a plasma-screen TV. But this is just as cool. Any high-res photo can be transformed into an amazing lit window showing the world of your choosing. Goodbye nightlight, hello wonder-world—I mean, light box.

DIFFICULTY LEVEL:
Super-challenging

TIME INVOLVED:
A weekend

MATERIALS:

20-×-25-inch backlight print (made from a photo from your collection and turned into a backlight print at a copy shop—more on this in the instructions)

8-foot 1×6 redwood board

Two ⅛-inch Plexiglas sheets cut to 20 × 25 inches (1 white sheet, 1 clear)

2-foot 1×6 redwood board

Two 24-inch fluorescent shop lights (these should have two bulbs each and measure 9 × 24 inches)

¾-inch MDF sheet cut to 19½ × 24½ inches

8-feet electrical outlet cord

Four 24-inch cool white fluorescent bulbs, a.k.a. T8 bulbs

FASTENERS:

Wood glue

2-inch finishing nails (20)

1½-inch wood screws (8)

1½-inch carriage bolts with nuts and washers (4 sets)

Red or yellow (these are sized by color; red and yellow sizes will both fit 14-gauge wire) wire nuts (2)

TOOLS:

Table saw

Hammer (or a nail gun, if you've got one)

Can of compressed air

Dish soap, water, and soft terry cloth to clean Plexiglas

Painter's tape

Drill with Phillips-head and ¼-inch and ⅛-inch bits

Wire stripper

Electrical tape

Chop saw

Socket wrench with ½-inch socket

INSTRUCTIONS:

1 First find a photo that will look good as a backlight print. Open it in your favorite image-editing program and make sure it has a resolution of 3000×3750 to 6000×7500 pixels (150 to 300 pixels per inch) when you resize it to 20 × 25 inches. (The higher the resolution, the higher the quality of the print will be; 150 pixels per inch will work fine, though, for something that will be seen from across the room.) Then put it on a flash drive or disk, take it to the copy shop, and have them make a backlight print. While that's being done, let's get started on the light box construction.

2 Using the chop saw, let's cut the pieces that form the sides of the box itself. For these we'll use the 8-foot 1×6 redwood. These pieces will have a 45°, mitered edge that falls across the 1-inch side. Cut two pieces that measure 19½ inches between the inside mitered edges. These will be the **SHORT LIGHT BOX SIDES**.

3 Cut two more pieces with the same miter that measure 24½ inches between the inside mitered edges. These will be the **LONG LIGHT BOX SIDES**. See image **a**.

4 Now let's move all four of our **LIGHT BOX SIDES** to the table saw. Place the fence ½ inch from the blade. Now set the blade so it's ¼ inch above the surface of the table. Cut a groove down the length of the insides the **LIGHT BOX SIDES**. (Make sure that the insides of the mitered edges are face down on the table saw and that the wood is flush against the fence.) See image **b**.

5 Move the fence away from the blade ¹⁄₁₆ inch and rip all the boards again. We want to end up with a ¼-inch groove. If your table saw blade is ¹⁄₁₆ inch, you'll need to move the fence and rip each board four times. The Plexiglas will rest in this groove. See image **c**.

6 Grab a **SHORT** and a **LONG LIGHT BOX SIDE** and line them up edge to edge, forming a corner and making sure the grooves match. Glue both edges and attach with five finishing nails spaced 1 inch apart.

7 Attach the other **SHORT LIGHT BOX SIDE** in the same way to form three sides of the box. Again, make sure the groove lines up. Lay the box on its side with the **SHORT SIDES** up in the air.

8 Has the copy shop finished your backlight print yet? If so, go get it and bring it back. Are you back? Okay, great. Make sure the print and the two sheets of Plexiglas are perfectly clean. Blow any dust off with compressed air, and clean the Plexiglas, if necessary, with mild dish soap, water, and a soft cloth. (Don't use ammonia-based glass cleaners or paper towels.) When everything is clean and dry, sandwich the print between the two sheets of Plexiglas, keeping the white sheet toward the inside of the box. Make sure that everything is flush so that no light will escape around the edges of the print.

9 Now slide the Plexiglas/backlight-print sandwich down into the groove of the wooden box, making sure that the correct side of the print is facing outward. Once it's in place, hold the two open sides of the box together with painter's tape. See image **d**.

10 Grab the remaining **LONG LIGHT BOX SIDE** and attach it to the rest of the light box as we did in Step 6.

11 Find the 2-foot 1×6 board and cut it in half lengthwise. These will be our **BACK STOPS**. The back of the light box will rest on these **BACK STOPS**.

12 Make sure your work surface is clean and lay the light box photo-side down. We're going to attach our **BACK**

a

b

c

d

e

STOPS to the inside of the LONG LIGHT BOX SIDES. Center the BACK STOP on the LONG LIGHT BOX SIDE so it's ¾ inch from what will be the back edge of the box. Drive a 1½-inch wood screw into the middle of each BACK STOP, 2 inches from each end.

13 Place the two shop lights down on the MDF board so they touch lengthwise. They should be ¾ inch from the long side of the MDF and ¼ inch from the short side.

14 When the lights are lined up, drill a ¼-inch hole through each mounting hole in the housing. Each housing should have two mounting holes. See image **e**.

15 Drill another hole in the MDF 1 inch away from the midpoint of the 24½-inch side. This will be where the power cord exits the light box.

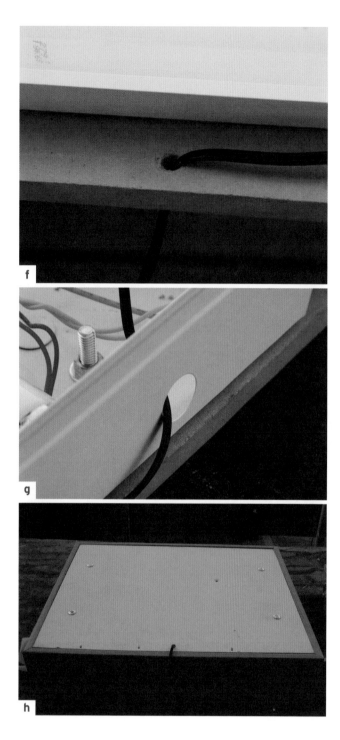

16 Now we need to drill four ⅛-inch mounting holes in the MDF. Put one ½ inch from each 24½-inch side, 6 inches from each end. See image **f**.

17 Insert a carriage bolt into each mounting hole from the underside of the MDF and secure to the shop-light housing using a nut and washer and socket wrench.

18 Insert the electrical cord (make sure it's nowhere near an outlet) through its hole, making sure that the plug will be on the outside of the box. Snake it a few inches through the hole in the end of the nearest housing. See images **f** and **g**.

19 Separate the end of the electrical cord into two strands and strip the ends to expose the wire. Look for two black wires coming out of the lights. Strip the ends of these and, using a wire nut, connect them both to the strand of the power cord that has writing on it. Tape the wire nut and wires together using a few inches of electrical tape.

20 Strip the ends of the white wires and the other power cord wire and connect them together the same way.

21 Insert all four bulbs, test, and then unplug the cord. Did they light up? Great! If they didn't, check the connections.

22 Place the lights inside the box by resting the MDF on the **BACK STOPS**. Make sure that the photo is right-side up relative to the power cord coming out of the back of the box.

23 Drive a 1½-inch wood screw into each of the ⅛-inch holes in the MDF to assemble the box. See image **h**.

24 Now hang it on your kid's wall as you would any other heavy picture, or just set it on your kid's desk. Turn off the lights and plug in the light box. Pretty awesome, huh?

HALF-PIPE

Are your kids having trouble finding places to skate? Are they tired of being hassled by cops and guys in golf shirts? Maybe that sick drainage culvert is just too far away, or maybe they just would like to have a dedicated spot to hit between urban-jungle sessions. If you have some space at your place, a half-pipe is the answer (and nothing beats building it yourself). To make things even better, I designed it to come apart in three sections (two ramps and a runway). That means it'll be easy easier to move out of the way when the driveway needs to fulfill its non-skate-and-destroy obligations (like parking access to the garage). Other than that, your house will be the new kid hot spot. Build it and they will come!

DIFFICULTY LEVEL:
Super-challenging

TIME INVOLVED:
A weekend

MATERIALS:

Two 4×8 sheets ¾-inch plywood subflooring

Thirty 8-foot 2×4 Douglas fir boards

Twelve 2×4 Douglas fir boards, pressure-treated
(Use gloves whenever you touch treated lumber.)

Twelve 4-foot-×-8-inch sheets ½-inch AC plywood
(AC plywood is smooth on one side.)
Alternative: Six 4-foot-×-8-inch sheets ½-inch "Skatelite."
(Skatelite can be found at www.skatelite.com in three colors: asphalt, dirt, and natural.)

Two 1½-inch-×-8-foot galvanized metal pipes

FASTENERS:

3-inch wood screws (500-count box)

TOOLS:

Measuring tape

String

Pencil

Circular saw with new blade

Chop saw (optional)

Drill with a Phillips-head bit, a 2-inch and a 3-inch long one, and ³⁄₁₆-inch and ¼-inch high-speed steel bits

Chalk line

Water

Broom

1 Let's start with the sidewalls of the half pipe. Grab a sheet of the ¾-inch subflooring and lay it down horizontally in front you. From the upper left-hand corner, measure 16 inches across the 8-foot side and make a mark. (Consult **Half-Pipe Cutting Guide** for this and the next couple of steps.)

2 From the lower left-hand corner measure 6 feet 6 inches across the other 8-foot side. Now put a mark 3½ inches vertically above the one you just made.

3 Now lay the end of the measuring tape on the lower edge of the subflooring right at the 6-foot 6-inch mark and measure vertically (in line with the 3½-inch mark) to a point 5 feet 9 inches away. This point will be off the plywood.

4 Attach a string at this point—I used vice grips and a wood screw. See image **a**. Tie a pencil to the other end of the string, so that its tip is at the 3½-inch mark you made. Now swing an arc on the plywood with the pencil that connects the 3½-inch mark with the 16-inch mark at the top edge of the sheet. See images **b** and **c**.

5 Cut out this shape with your circular saw. This will be your template for the next three cuts in the ¾-inch ply. See image **d**.

6 Now rotate the sidewall piece you just cut onto the leftover plywood. Make sure the square edges are flush, trace the curve, and cut it out. You'll have a surfboard-shaped leftover. Are you thinking about building some kind of two-person surfing simulator? Great! You'll have another surfboard-shaped leftover from the next step.

7 Use the same template to trace the shape, twice, onto the other sheet of ¾-inch subflooring. Cut out both pieces. You should now have four identical sidewalls.

8 On all four sidewalls, cut a 1-×-1-inch notch out of the corner where the 16-inch top section meets the transition (the curved part of the sidewall). See image **e**.

9 Cut 28 of the non-treated 2×4 pieces to 94½ inches. I stacked them three-high on the chop saw, made sure the ends were flush, and cut them simultaneously. Make sure they're all exactly the same length!

10 Cut 10 of the pressure-treated 2×4 pieces to 93 inches and leave the other two 8 feet long.

11 Now we're going to trace the positions of the joists on the outside of the sidewall. Make a mark on the very edge of the transition ¾ inch from the corner where it meets the 3½-inch side. Now grab a cut-off piece of 2×4 timber and place it vertically at the bottom of the transition against one of the sidewalls, flush up against the 3½-inch edge. Trace the position of the 2×4 timber onto the sidewall. The mark you made on the edge of the transition will be the centerline for the joist we will attach shortly. Transfer the on-center mark to the scrap 2×4 timber. See **Transferring the On-Center Mark**.

12 Starting from the on-center mark you just made, make a mark on that same edge every 8 inches as you move up the transition to the top of the ramp. You should end up with a total of 10 marks.

13 Line up all four transitions perfectly and transfer the marks to the other three edges.

14 Now let's mark the positions of all the joists on the outside of the sidewalls using that scrap piece of 2×4 timber. Center the mark on the scrap with the mark on the transition, making sure both edges are flush against each other. See image **f**.

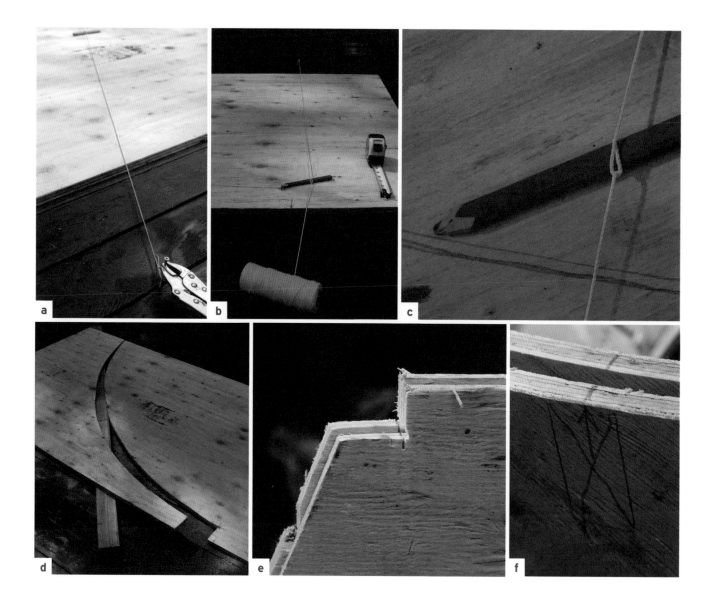

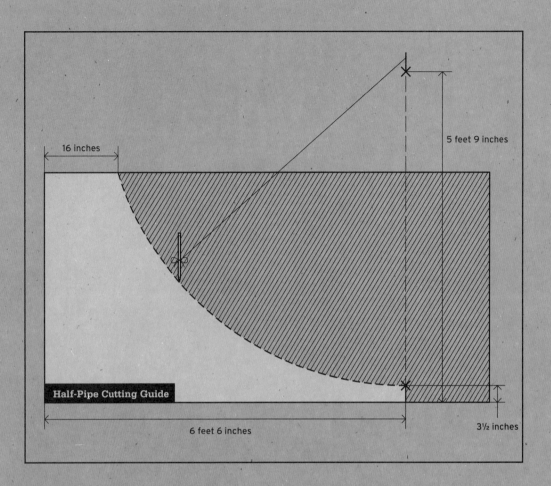

16 inches

5 feet 9 inches

Half-Pipe Cutting Guide

6 feet 6 inches

3½ inches

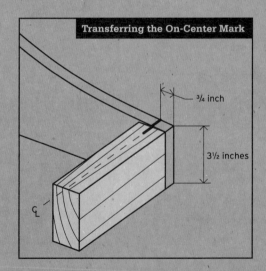

Transferring the On-Center Mark

¾ inch

3½ inches

C_L

15 When you get to a 1-×-1-inch notch, lay the wide side of the 2×4 timber flush against the transition, tuck the corner into the notch, and then trace it. See image **g**.

16 Place the scrap piece vertically flush against the top edge of the sidewall and the 1-×-1-inch notch. Trace it and mark the centerline on the top edge of the sidewall. From that centerline, measure 7 inches in back along the top of the sidewall and make another centerline. Now place the scrap 2×4 timber vertically in the top back corner and trace it again. The three joists will support the top of the ramp. See image of top of ramp in Step 25 to see where these marks go.

17 Trace another outline of the 2×4 timber vertically into the bottom rear corner of the sidewall. Make sure all these 2×4 timber outlines appear (and are the same) on the rest of the sidewalls.

18 Now we'll start attaching the joists to the sidewalls. (At this point it would be great to have a helper. I mention this elsewhere in the book, but I'll reiterate it here.) Every 2×4 timber has a "crown," that is, the shorter side will bow out along its length. As we build the half-pipe, we want to make sure that these bows or crowns are facing up. Start with the two outermost bottom joists, driving two wood screws through the sidewalls into the ends of each. Make sure you line up the ends with the pencil marks on the outside of sidewall. See image **h**. Next do the joists at the top edge and follow the transition down, adding joists where they're outlined on the sidewalls. Continue using two wood screws per end and keep the crowns facing up. See image **i**. When you get to the point in the transition that's 4 feet away from the top of the ramp (as measured along the edge of the sidewall) double up the beams. This is how far the first piece of plywood will reach, so there'll be a seam there later on. We'll want each piece of ply meeting at this seam to be supported by a joist, so make sure you put one exactly on either side of the 4-foot mark. Do the same for the other ramp. See image **j**.

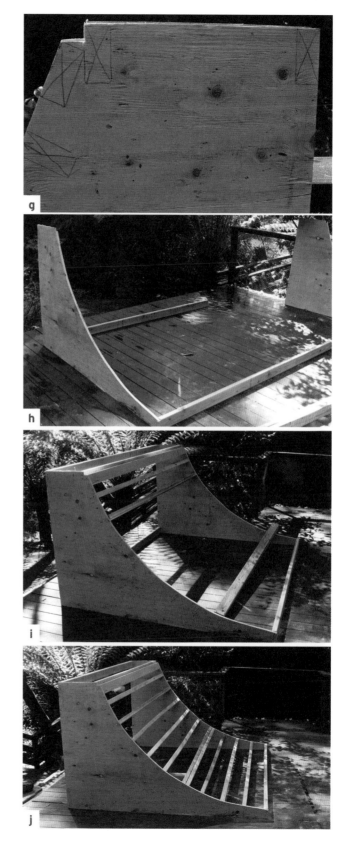

g

h

i

j

19 Okay, let's move on to the runway, which is the middle section. This will be a perfect 8-×-8-foot square. To start, grab the two original-length, pressure-treated 2×4 pieces and lay them down parallel to each other, about 93 inches apart.

20 Lay two of the ten 93-inch-long 2×4 pieces down perpendicularly between the ends of the long 2×4 pieces from the last step to form a square. Lay the remaining 2×4 pieces down similarly, spaced 12 inches on-center, except at the 4-foot mark. There, lay a 2×4 timber on either side of the 4-foot mark to support the edge of the plywood sheet that we'll be attaching later. Attach these two 2×4 pieces together using six wood screws. As for the rest of it, you know the drill: two wood screws in each end. Try to get them on the centerline of the end of each beam. This will help in the next step. See image **k**. Here's a tip: Before you drive all of the screws, make sure the runway is square. To do that, measure diagonally from corner to corner in both directions. If the two measurements match, you're all squared up.

21 Place two sheets of ½-inch plywood side-by-side on the runway, smooth side up. Make sure the two edges butting up against each other line up with the edges of the two 2×4 timbers straddling the 4-foot mark. When all the edges are lined up, attach the plywood to the runway by driving one wood screw into the frame every 24 inches. Use a chalk line to mark the centerlines of the 2×4 pieces.

A couple of things: Promise me you're going to countersink all of the screws on the deck ¹⁄₁₆ inch by setting your drill to "Slow/Torque" and really pressing to get the screws to sink in. This pipe will be monumentally great if you make it smooth. Trust me. You don't want some wise-guy screw sticking its head under your kids' wheels or, worse, slicing up their skin. This will be part of your quality control. The same goes for any movement or soft spots that develop. Fix them right away. They'll only come back to bite when everyone least expects it, like when your kid's new girlfriend or boyfriend is watching and their friends are rolling video. The last thing they'll want to do then is stack. There are better things to be known for on YouTube.

k   l   m

22 Lay another two sheets of ½-inch plywood on the runway so that the butt seam on these sheets is perpendicular to the ones underneath. When all is said and done, we want the grain on the top layer of plywood to be parallel to the direction your kids will be skating. If it's not, rotate the runway so that it is. Are your kids and their friends just sitting around waiting for you to finish? Get them to help. They're on the skate construction crew. Now mark the centerlines of the 2×4 pieces again and drive a wood screw into these beams every 12 inches, offsetting your screw pattern so that you don't hit the screws underneath. Driving so many screws may seem like overkill, but you'll thank me next year when this ramp is still rock solid. See image **l**.

23 Alright, let's go ahead and install the 1½-inch metal pipes to form the lip of each ramp. We'll start by drilling a line of ³⁄₁₆-inch holes all the way through the pipes. Measure from one end and drill a hole every 12 inches, making sure they form a straight line. Drill one more hole on each end, in line with the others, 2 inches from the end of the pipe. Now drill the holes on one side of the pipe out to ¼ inch. This will enable the heads of the screws to go though one side of the pipe but not the other.

24 Lay the pipe into the notched pocket at the top of the ramp, rotating it so the holes are oriented at a 45° angle into the corner, with the ¼-inch holes on the outside. Now secure it using the 3-inch wood screws. You'll be drilling into the 2×4 piece on the upper part of the ramp. See image **m**. Repeat these last two steps for the other ramp. Okay, we're getting closer to skate time!

25 Now let's work on the transitions. Grab your skater construction crew and a sheet of ½-inch ply, head down to the creek, and toss it in. Give it a good soak. Be sure to hang on to it—there's no need to send free building materials downstream. What's that? No creek nearby? No worries. Just give the plywood a good soak with a water hose. When it's soaked and done dripping, lay the longest edge flush against the metal rail and drive in a wood screw ¾ inch from the top edge, on the centerline of the ramp, to hold it in place—¾ inch will put you in the middle of the 2×4 piece underneath. Then drive wood screws along that same edge, every 12 inches. Now mark the centerline of the next 2×4 joist with your chalk line and drive

wood screws in at 12-inch intervals. Wetting the wood helps, but it's still not going to be easy to bend the plywood into place. The first rungs will be the hardest. Just put weight on the ply and move down joist by joist, or have your skate construction crew tilt the ramp on its back to more directly apply their weight to the first few rungs. Oh, don't paint the lip, either. It'll just make it slippery and everyone will stack for sure. See images **n** and **o**.

26 To fill in the remaining section of the ramp, measure the distance from the edge of the plywood to the bottom edge of the ramp. Mark this distance on another piece of ½-inch plywood and snap a chalk line to mark the cut. Make sure you cut it really straight. Use another piece of plywood as a guide, if that helps. This piece of plywood should be about 31½ inches wide, but measure it so you get a precise fit.

27 Push the ramps and runway together so they're flush. Cut two 2×4 timbers in half and lay the resulting 4-foot boards against both sides of the half-pipe, evenly over-

n o p

lapping the seam where the sections meet, 2 feet on each side of the seam. Use four wood screws per board in a zigzag pattern to tie the sections together. See image **p**.

28 Alright, now let's lay down the second layer of plywood. In order to make a world-class ramp, use "Skatelite" for the final layer. Simply apply the same way you would the plywood (there is no "grain" so no need to worry about the direction). This step will separate the men from the boys, since the grain on these sheets should be parallel to the fall of the ramp. (The "fall" is the direction a ball would roll if it fell on the ramp.) Really soak it and then do a test. Get your skate construction crew to stand on it. (Not in the middle! Start at an edge.) Will it bend to the form of the ramps? If it just won't work, lay it down with the grain perpendicular to the ramp. Either way, cut two sheets of ply to fit, and start attaching them from the bottom edge this time, driving one wood screw every 12 inches and lining them up with the 2×4 joists as before. The seam, where this sheet of plywood butts up against the runway, should be perfect. You shouldn't even be able to feel it. Makes sure you countersink these screws. If you were able to bend the wood so the grain is parallel to the fall of the ramp, you'll need two pieces of

ply that measure about 4 × 6 feet. If you laid the grain down perpendicularly, you'll need a standard 4-×-8-foot sheet and a 31½-inch sheet. These are just rough numbers. Measure in either case to get the best fit. Complete both ramps.

29 Cut four pieces of ½-inch plywood measuring 15 inches × 8 feet and install two layers of each at the top of each ramp. Snap a chalk line to mark the centers of the joists underneath, and drive a wood screw every 12 inches along each centerline. For the second layer, shift the 12-inch screw pattern 6 inches over to avoid hitting the screws on the first layer.

30 Now give everyone in the skate construction crew a broom. The half-pipe needs a final dust-off.

31 Look at that! You built a half-pipe! Way to go! Your kids can now grab their decks, run up to the top of the ramp, yell "Dropping!" and drop in. The half-pipe is open! I think it's fair to say that your kids and their friends will now be skating until they can't skate anymore. By the way, your kids' friends, they're good kids? You like them? Great—you'll be seeing a lot more of them now.

ROPE BRIDGE

Nothing shouts "jungle adventure" quite like a rickety rope bridge slung across a canyon of doom. Who wouldn't want to try to cross, heart pounding, while avoiding the treacheries below. Snapping crocodiles? A raging river? Or both! The bridge looks as old as the hills. Will it hold? Your kids have no choice but to try—a thundering herd of rhinoceroses is right behind them! They make a run for it, but the wind picks up and the bridge begins to sway! They hang on for dear life! Must . . . make it . . . to . . . the . . . other . . . side. But with the next step, a rotting rung collapses and falls away, only to disappear hundreds of feet below! Will they make it? Ahhhhh!!! Who knows! One thing's for certain, though: This bridge packs all of same thrills but is safe and strong enough to ensure many years of backyard adventures.

DIFFICULTY LEVEL:
Super-challenging

TIME INVOLVED:
A weekend

MATERIALS:

100 feet ¼-inch steel cable

12 feet garden hose

Twelve 8-foot 2×6 redwood or pressure-treated lumber boards

600 feet 1½-inch hemp rope

Black spray paint

Scrap 2×4 timber (enough to form a ladder on the trees for bridge access)

FASTENERS:

¾-inch U-bolts (12)

2½-inch U-bolts (100)

3-inch wood screws (about 50)

TOOLS:

Cable cutters, hacksaw, or electric saw with a metal-cutting blade

Strong duct tape

Utility knife

Socket wrench with socket that fits U bolts

Twine (as a construction guide)

Level

Drill with ¼-inch bit

Chop saw or circular saw

NOTE: For details on tying the knots referred to in this project, refer to the Knots section on page 162.

INSTRUCTIONS:

1 Find two trees at least 10 inches in diameter and about 30 feet apart from one another. You can make the bridge shorter or longer (up to 60 feet), depending on the amount of material you're willing to use. These instructions assume a 30-foot span.

2 Cut the steel cable into two pieces 50 feet long. Tightly wrap duct tape around both ends so the cable doesn't fray.

3 Using your utility knife, cut the garden hose into four equal-length pieces.

4 Insert one end of one of the cable pieces into a piece of garden hose, pushing it through so you have about 4 feet of cable sticking out the other side.

5 Find a spot on the first tree where the trunk forms a Y. Ideally this spot should be 6 to 10 feet off the ground, and the opening between limb and trunk should be 2 to 3 feet wide. Wrap the cable around the tree so only the garden hose section—not the actual cable—touches it. This will prevent the cable from damaging the tree after years of bridge crossings.

6 Now attach the cable to itself using three ¾-inch U-bolts. Place the first one 2 inches from the end of the garden hose, and space the other two at 3-inch intervals. Adjust the cable so about 1 foot of it extends past the last U-bolt, then tighten down all of the U-bolts with the socket wrench. See image **a**.

7 Attach the other end of the cable to the other tree in the same way, at the same height, making sure you have 12 to 18 inches of sag at the midpoint of the cable before tightening the U-bolts. To check this, tie a length of twine tautly between the two trees at the same points that the cable is attached to. At the midpoint of the twine and cable, you can measure the sag.

8 Attach the second cable to the trees about 2 feet from, and parallel to, the first. Leave one end of the cable loose so that you can make adjustments.

9 Place your level across the two cables at their midpoints and adjust the length of the second cable from the loose end until the cable's midpoints are level with each other. Now go ahead and tighten down the last set of U-bolts.

10 Cut the 2×6 lumber into 2-foot-long pieces. You'll want 50 of these. We'll use them as bridge treads.

11 We'll attach the wooden bridge treads to the cable using the 2½-inch U-bolts. Start by making a template to drill the holes for the U-bolts. First cut some thin scrap wood to the same size as the tread and draw a centerline on it lengthwise. Mark the positions for the bolt holes so the middles of the U-bolts will be centered on the line 3 inches from each edge and their bolts will be in line with the centerline. See image **b**. Drill holes into all the treads using the same template to ensure consistency. See **Making the Tread Template**.

12 Attach the first bridge tread as close to the tree as possible. To do this, drop U-bolts into the holes you've drilled in the tread. Place them so that each set of bolts is straddling one of the cables. See image **c**. Attach the U-bolt and tighten the nuts. Keep tightening the nuts until the top of the U-bolt sinks into, and becomes flush with, the top of the tread.

13 Attach the rest of the treads the same way, leaving a gap of 2 inches between each one. (Use a 2-inch spacer piece to ensure all the gaps are equal.)

14 Cut two pieces of rope 50 feet long. You're going to attach these to the tree at the spots where the cables attach. Start by wrapping each piece of rope around the

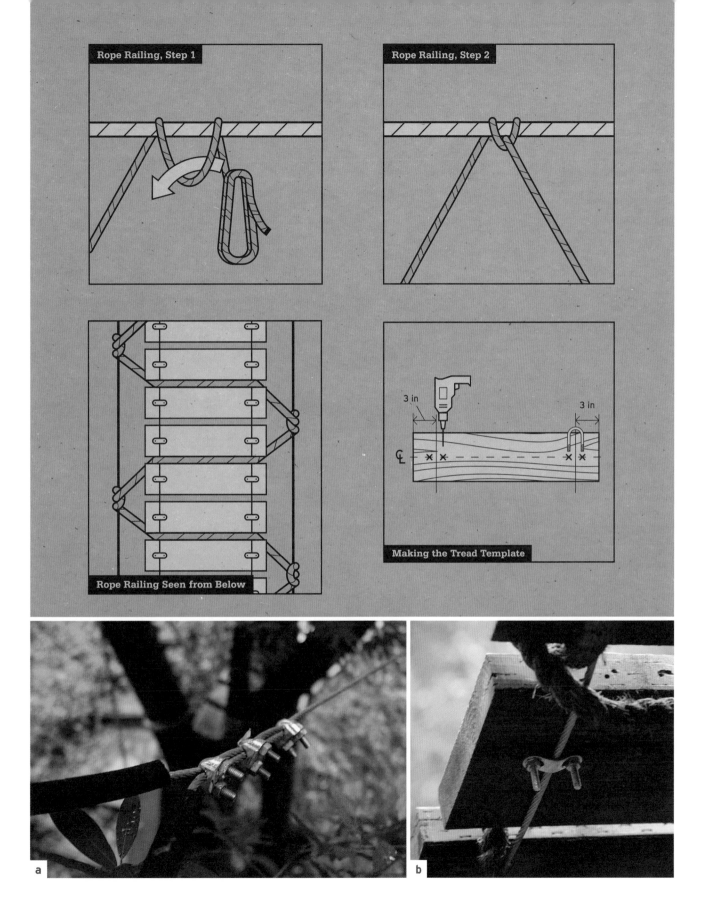

Rope Railing, Step 1

Rope Railing, Step 2

Rope Railing Seen from Below

Making the Tread Template

3 in

3 in

C̵L

a

b

tree three times, leaving 4 feet or so of "tail," and then follow the instructions for tying a fisherman's bend.

15 Weave the standing part of the rope over and under every tread along the path of each cable. See image **c**. The cable will be supporting the weight of the bridge, but this makes it look like it's the rope that's doing all the work. When you get to the other side, make another fisherman's bend. Do what you like with the excess rope on either end—wrap it around the tree, fray the ends, or do both to give the bridge a rough, adventurous look.

16 Now it's time to make the railing. Cut another two pieces of rope 50 feet long. This will give you about 10 feet of rope on either side with which to tie the knots and add any extra decorative touches. Using a fisherman's bend, tie one piece of the rope to the tree about 4 feet above the point where one of the cables is attached. Tie the same knot on the other tree, ensuring that the rope droops to about 3½ inches above the treads at the bridge's midpoint.

17 Do the same thing with the rope on the other side, but when you string the railing across to the opposite tree, tie a temporary knot. Then lay your level across the railings at the midpoint and tie the final fisherman's bend once you've adjusted the level of the railings.

18 Grab the remaining rope (about 400 feet). Tie another fisherman's bend on the tree above the railing. This is where things get a little tricky. We're going to create a wall of rope between the deck of the bridge and the railings. To do that, we'll weave the rope between the treads and the railing, switching from side to side as the rope passes under the bridge.

19 To start, weave the rope under the first tread. Then come up and form a bight over the railing. Lay the bight over the top of the railing and pass remaining rope through it. See **Rope Railing, Steps 1** and **2** to get a sense of how this works. See image **d**. Skip two treads and pass the rope down again between treads three and four. Now pass the rope to the other side of the bridge, bring it up to wrap around the opposite railing, skip two treads, pass the rope back under the bridge, and so on. See **Rope Railing Seen from Below**. When you reach the opposite end of the bridge, tie the rope off above the railing on whichever tree is most convenient. See image **e**.

20 You've done it! Now do some safety testing by jumping around on the bridge to make sure all the connections are secure. Start cautiously at first! Then, with the spray paint, paint all of the exposed metal hardware black.

21 Cut some scrap 2×4 timbers into 8-inch lengths to form a ladder for access to the bridge. Attach each rung to the tree using three 3-inch wood screws screwed into the center of each rung in a triangular pattern. Tie up all the excess rope. For a final touch, add extra bits of rope and wood to give the bridge an aged, well-worn look. Now dare the adventurous to cross!

c d e

CIRCUS TENT

The circus is in town, and guess where the big top is? That's right—a room in your house! There's no need to buy tickets, and the show can run as long as you like. Whether you're into circuses, puppet shows, rock concerts, or theater, they can all happen at your very own tent venue. Just break out the peanuts and pink popcorn, cue the music, and have your kids invite all of their friends over for the best show ever!

DIFFICULTY LEVEL:
Super-challenging

TIME INVOLVED:
A weekend

One quick note: These directions assume you have a framed window 64 inches wide or less, and 9-foot ceilings or higher. If you have 8-foot ceilings, shorten the main wood supports, curtains, and main tent fabric lengths by 12 inches.

MATERIALS:

17 yards 60-inch-wide red velvet (or other heavy fabric of your choice) for the outer part of the tent

10 yards 60-inch-wide fun, patterned fabric (in a similar color) for the inside of the tent

Thread, in a similar color (1 spool)

1 quart paint (or spray paint) to match your fabric

1½-inch-×-6-foot pine pole for curtain rod

Four 8-foot 2×4 Douglas fir boards

Two 10-foot 2×4 Douglas fir boards

6-foot 1×6 redwood or pine board

8-foot 1×8 pine board

12-inch-×-16-foot roll of Hollofil

FASTENERS:

Large safety pins (20)

2-inch-wide Velcro strip
(12 inches each of the rough and fuzzy sides)

Wood glue

7d finishing nails (10)

2-inch L bracket with four 1-inch wood screws (4 sets)

½-inch heavy-duty staples (500-count box)

3-inch wood screws (50-count box)

½-×-7-inch lag bolt with washer (2)

2½-inch hook and eye latch (1)

TOOLS:

Sewing machine

Paintbrush

Chop saw

Hammer

Heavy-duty stapler

Table saw

Carpenter's square

Drafting compass (optional)

Jigsaw with multipurpose blade

Drill, with ⅜-×-6-inch, ⅛-inch, and Phillips-head bits

Stud finder

Pencil

Level

6-foot ladder

Socket wrench with ¾-inch socket

INSTRUCTIONS:

1 Cut 8 yards of the outer and inner fabrics.

2 Sew them together, back-to-back, so the good sides are both facing out. See images **a** and **b**.

3 Now we're going to sew a 4-inch hem into the short sides. Fold the fabric over 2 inches so that the inner fabric is on the inside of the fold. Now fold it over again, 4 inches this time. Pin the fabric with large safety pins (it's really thick) and sew the hem ½ inch from the first fold. (Don't sew over the safety pins.) Do this for both sides. When this piece is finished, it will form the walls and ceiling of the tent. We'll call this the **MAIN TENT**. See image **c**. Fold this piece and set it aside.

4 From the outer fabric, cut two pieces measuring 9 feet 6 inches long.

5 Along the long sides of each piece, fold 1 inch of the better side of the fabric onto the back and sew a hem. You'll sew four seams total. These pieces will form the curtains at the front of the tent.

6 Make an 8-inch fold from front to back in one of the short sides of each curtain and hem them together. These will be the loops in the tops through which the curtain rod will go.

7 Again, folding the good side toward the back, make a 4-inch hem in the bottom edge of both the curtains. Alright, the curtains are done! These are gonna be great! Fold and set them aside.

8 From the inner fabric, cut two 13-x-36-inch pieces. These will be the tiebacks for the curtains.

9 Fold these pieces in half lengthwise, with the good side in, and sew each piece together ½ inch from the long, open edge. Now turn them inside out again. You should have what look like two sleeves with a clean seam and the fun pattern on the outside.

10 Now lay these flat so that the seam is in the middle of one side. Fold one end over ½ inch toward the seam, then another 2 inches, and hem together. Do this for the other piece too.

11 Now cut the Velcro strip into two 6-inch pieces. Peel them apart and sew a fuzzy-sided strip onto each 2-inch sash hem. Stick the other sides of the Velcro back on for now. We'll come back to these later. The Velcro will make it really quick and easy to hold the curtains back.

12 Moving on to the other end of the tiebacks, make a ½-inch fold and hem both pieces. See image **d**.

13 Paint all of the wood pieces (except for the 1×8) your chosen color. See image **e**. Let them dry overnight.

14 Good morning! How early is it? Is it early enough to use a chop saw? Great! Then cut all of the 8-foot-long 2×4 timbers down to 69 inches. (Whoops—I meant is it late enough? Sorry, neighbors!)

15 Cut the 10-foot-long 2×4 timbers down to 8 feet 6 inches. These will be the **MAIN SUPPORT** posts.

16 From the 8-foot 1×8 board, cut a piece that's 72 inches long, and two 12-inch-long pieces.

17 Butt both ends of the 72-inch piece against the sides of the 12-inch pieces (like you're forming three sides of a long narrow box). Attach them using wood glue and finishing nails. To make it sturdy, add a couple of L brackets, 1 inch from each edge, to each inside corner. See image **f**.

18 Congratulations. You've just made a valance.

19 Now let's cover the entire valance with Hollofil. Just double it up (fold it from 16 feet down to 8 feet), wrap it around the valance, and staple it in place. Start by stapling

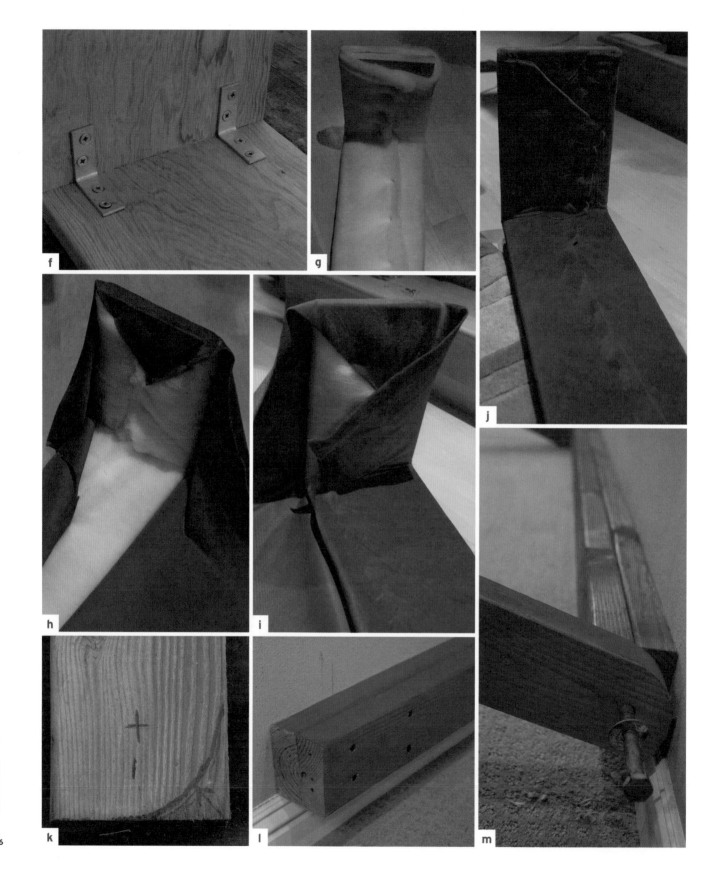

one side to the middle of the inside of the valance, then stretch the other side around to the middle and staple it. See image **g**.

20 Find the remaining piece of the outer fabric and lay it facedown. Now lay the valance on top of it, diagonally, with the sides pointing up. Stretch the corners of the fabric tightly over the ends of the valance and staple them down. Continue stretching and stapling the fabric onto the back of the valance, trimming and discarding the excess. See images **h**, **i**, and **j**.

21 Cut the curtain rod down to 71½ inches. Cutting it to a little less than 72 inches will allow room for the fabric and Hollofil when we install it in the valance later on.

22 Using your table saw, rip the 6-foot 1×6 timber lengthwise into one 2-inch-wide strip and two 1¾-inch-wide strips.

23 Cut the 2-inch-wide strip down to 68 inches and the two 1¾-inch strips down to 60 inches. The first one will be the **TOP STRIP** and the other two will be the **SIDE STRIPS**. I mitered the corners of my **TOP** and **SIDE STRIPS** where they meet. You can too, but it's not necessary.

24 Do you remember the **MAIN SUPPORT** posts from Step 15? Grab them and look for the "crown" in the beam. Every 2×4 timber bows a little, bulging on one of its narrow sides. This bow is known as the "crown." Sight down the length of the wood to see it. We want the crown to point away from the wall. We'll also round off the bottom corner of the wall-facing side of the **SUPPORT** so it doesn't scrape the wall when it rotates forward. To do this, draw a line across the wide side of the beam 1¾ inches from the bottom edge, using your carpenter's square. Now draw a line a 2 inches up the center of the board. (The center happens to be 1¾ inches from either edge.) Place the point of your drafting compass where these two lines cross and a draw a 1¾-inch radius curve across the corner. See image **k**. Trim this curve off with a jigsaw. Do the same for the other **MAIN SUPPORT** beam.

HERE'S A LITTLE TIP: If you don't have a drafting compass, tap a finishing nail into the mark and tie a string around it and a pencil, leaving 1¾ inches between the two. That'll work just as well.

25 Now drill a ⅜-inch hole where the lines meet. Repeat these two steps for the other **MAIN SUPPORT** post.

26 Using the stud finder, mark all of the studs above and below the window where you're setting up the tent.

27 Take one of the 69-inch 2×4 boards and mount it just above the baseboard trim, on center with the window. It should protrude beyond the edges of the window frame by 2½ inches on each side. There should be at least three studs in the wall under the window. Predrill two holes through the 2×4 stud and then drive a 3-inch wood screw into each hole. Bury the screws deep—this needs to be strong.

28 Place another 69-inch 2×4 board flush in front of the one you just placed. Attach it using 3-inch wood screws in groups of two in an over-and-under pattern. Drive a set of screws in 2 inches from each end, 8 inches from each end, and another set right in the middle. See image **l**. Let's call this the **LOWER RAIL**.

29 You may need an assistant for these next two steps. Hold the side of the rounded end of one of the **MAIN SUPPORTS** against one end of the **LOWER RAIL** so the top of the **SUPPORT** is pointed away from the wall. The rounded end shouldn't touch the wall, because it needs to rotate. Put a lag bolt through the hole using the socket wrench in the **SUPPORT** to test the rotation. If everything looks good, give the lag bolt a little tap with a hammer to mark the spot. Measure the mark and put one in the same location on the other end of the **LOWER RAIL**. See image **m**.

30 Drill a ⅜-inch hole 6 inches deep into the first mark you made with the lag bolt. Be sure to drill straight into the end of the **LOWER RAIL**. Don't let the drill drift at an angle. Do the same for the other side.

31 Grab the remaining two 69-inch 2×4 pieces, line them up flush with one another, and attach them together using four 3-inch wood screws evenly spaced lengthwise. This will be the **TOP RAIL**.

32 Line up the **TOP RAIL** between the tops of the **MAIN SUPPORTS**. When everything is flush, drive four wood screws into each end, two per 2×4 timber. I went for overkill and used six in image **n**, but four will do fine.

33 Line up the holes you made in the **MAIN SUPPORT** and the **LOWER RAIL** making sure the rounded corners of the **MAIN SUPPORT** are against the wall. Insert the ½-×-7-inch lag bolts, with washers, through each hole and drive them in until they're snug.

34 Now grab a pencil, a level, and the ladder and raise the **SUPPORT** so it's exactly vertical. Use the level to check. When it is, trace the inside of the **SUPPORT** onto the wall. Great—you can lay the **SUPPORT** back down.

35 Line up the **TOP STRIP** (2 × 68 inches) on the wall so that its top edge is flush with the line you just drew. It will overhang the vertical parts of your line by ½ inch on either side. Attach it to the wall using one 3-inch wood screw per stud (that you found in Step 26). Predrill with a ⅛-inch bit so you don't split the stud, then drive the screw. Do the outermost studs first. There should be about five of them total. See image **o**.

36 Now let's install the **SIDE STRIPS** (1¾ × 60 inches). Lay one so that it's flush with both the side of the window and the **TOP STRIP**. Attach it using three 3-inch wood screws—one 2 inches from each end, and one in the middle. Predrill with the ⅛-inch bit and drive them in at a 45° angle so that you hit the stud running vertically next to the window. See image **p**.

37 Fold the **MAIN SUPPORT** back up against the wall and attach the latch hook to the middle of the underside, 1 inch from the edge closest to the wall. Attach the eye of the latch in the middle of the **TOP STRIP**. This hook will hold the tent to the wall and keep the excess fabric from draping in front of the window. It will also keep tiny circus performers from starting the "most awesome show on earth" without you. See image **q**.

38 Make a line on the top of the **MAIN SUPPORT**, marking its midpoint. Do the same on the top edge of the **TOP STRIP**. Fold the **MAIN SUPPORT** back down for now.

39 Find the **MAIN TENT** from Step 3 and fold it in half lengthwise to find the midpoint. Mark it with a line on both edges, front and back, just dark enough so you can see it.

40 Now with the outer fabric of the **MAIN TENT** facing up, match its midpoint to the midpoint of the **TOP STRIP**. Staple it down. Continue stapling every 2 inches. Do this in both directions, and do the same for both **SIDE STRIPS**.

41 Line up the midpoint on the other side of the **MAIN TENT** with the midpoint on the top of the **MAIN SUPPORT**. Wrap the fabric over the top of the beam to form a ¾-inch lip on the front side. Staple every 2 inches along this lip of fabric in both directions, stopping at the ends of the horizontal beam.

42 Insert the wooden curtain rod through the 8-inch hem loops in each curtain. Make sure both curtains are facing the same way.

43 Now position the curtain rod in the valance so that the ends are centered at points 4½ inches back from the front and 2 inches down from the top on both sides. See image **r**. Drill one wood screw through the valance and into the curtain rod on each end. It may help to make a small cut in the valance fabric so that it doesn't twist up when you sink the screw.

44 Attach the valance to the top of the **MAIN SUPPORT** using three wood screws per side. Make sure the back and top of the valance is flush with the back and top of the **MAIN SUPPORT**, and that the **MAIN TENT** is between the **SUPPORT** and the valance.

45 Okay, we're getting close to finishing. Let's grab the curtain tiebacks from Step 12 and attach the non-Velcro ends to the **SIDE STRIPS**. We'll use staples. It'll look slick if you hide them. Here's how: Lay the tieback with what will be the outside edge against the wall. It should be 3 feet 6 inches from the floor, and the ½-inch hem should be against the **SIDE STRIP** and **MAIN TENT**. Press the staple gun flush against the wall and staple the tiebacks into the **SIDE STRIP**. Now fold it over and the staples will disappear. Do the same for the other side. See **Attaching Curtain Tieback 1** and **2**.

46 Fold and latch the tent against the wall. You'll have to push the ceiling of the **MAIN TENT** up a bit to expose the eye of the latch.

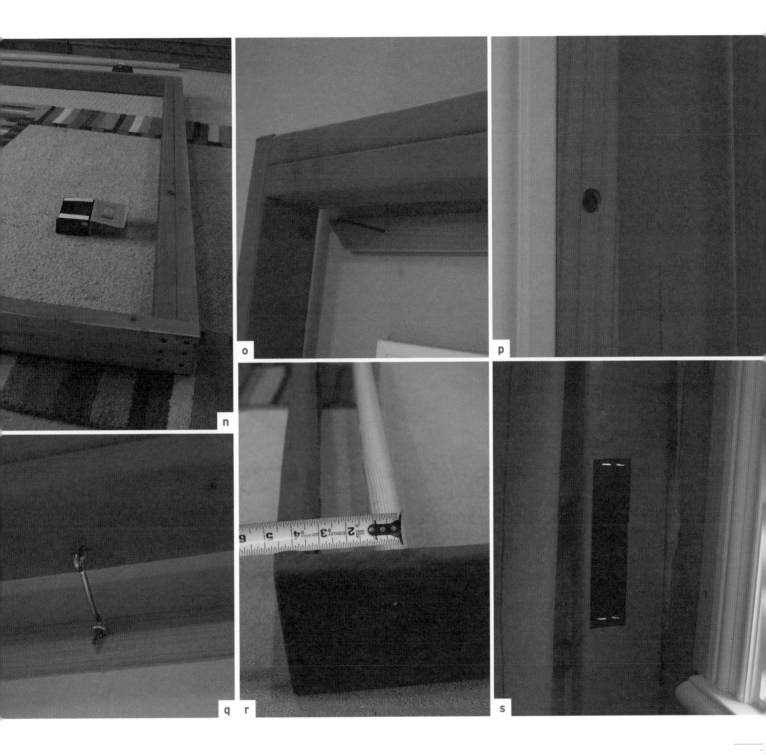

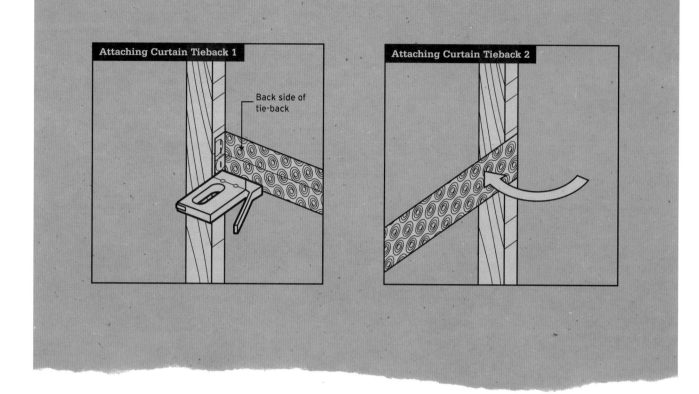

Attaching Curtain Tieback 1

Back side of
tie-back

Attaching Curtain Tieback 2

47 Wrap the tiebacks around the **MAIN TENT** fabric so the Velcro end lines up with the inside edge of the **MAIN SUPPORT**. Make sure both ends of the tiebacks are level with each other. Peel off the rough-sided Velcro and staple it to the inside of the **MAIN SUPPORT** at the edge farthest from the window. See image **s**.

48 Now attach the tiebacks to the **MAIN SUPPORT** and . . . you're done!

49 After a few rehearsals of your kids' big production, have them invite everyone over to take a seat for the show. When they wonder why they're staring at a window, lower the lights, fire up the spotlights, and unlatch the tent! Dah-da-daaahh! It's showtime!

GO-CART

Do you know someone who's itching to get behind the wheel of their own sweet ride but can't quite yet reach the pedals of a normal car? Maybe they want to get an early start on their racing career but can't yet see over the steering wheel? Well, for that little Mario Andretti, a go-cart is the perfect choice.

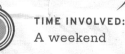

DIFFICULTY LEVEL:
Super-challenging

TIME INVOLVED:
A weekend

MATERIALS:

I use Ipe wood for this project (see the Skate Longboard project, page 74, for details). You could use redwood, but it's not as strong and may splinter. You could also use Douglas fir. It'd be cheaper but not as strong—but you would be able to make all of the connections with wood screws. I recommend Ipe wood, though. It looks great for a classic project like this and will stand up to years of abuse.

4-foot 1×7 Ipe wood board

10 feet ¾-×-5½-inch Ipe wood board

14 feet 1-×-5½-inch Ipe wood board

8-inch rubber wheels, preferably with metal hubs and bearings (or plastic-rimmed lawnmower wheels if you plan on losing every race you enter)

Super Lube, for the wheels

4 feet ¾-inch nylon rope

10-inch-wide grip tape (you'll need about 8 inches)

FASTENERS:

¼-×-2½-inch carriage bolts with matching washers and nuts (23 each)

¼-×-3½-inch carriage bolts with matching washers and nuts (4 each)

⅜-×-3-inch lag bolt with matching washers (2 each)

½-×-4½-inch carriage bolt (1), with matching washer, and 2 nuts for locking

12-×-2-inch oval-head, stainless-steel screws (28) (They must be stainless steel to have enough strength to use with Ipe wood.)

½-×-7½-inch galvanized lag bolts (4), with 16 matching washers (½ inch × 40 millimeters)

Duct tape

TOOLS:

Jigsaw

Chop saw

Carpenter's square

Pencil

Drill with the following spade bits:
¾ inch × 6 inches
⅝ inch × 6 inches
½ inch × 6 inches
⅜ inch × 6 inches

and the following bits:
¼ inch
¹¹⁄₆₄ inch

Mini clamps

Crescent wrench or ¾-inch box wrench

Socket wrench with the following sockets:
¾ inch
⁹⁄₁₆ inch
⁷⁄₁₆ inch

Electric sander with five sheets of 60-grit sandpaper

NOTE: For details on tying the knots referred to in this project, refer to the Knots section on page 162.

1 Start by cutting all of the pieces down to size. The 4-foot 1-×-7-inch piece is already just what we need. This will be the **FRAME** of the cart. Just round off one end with a jigsaw. See image **a**. Draw a centerline lengthwise down both faces of the board. We're going to end up with a lot of cut pieces, so label them lightly in pencil as we go to keep things organized.

2 From the 10-foot ¾-×-5½-inch Ipe wood board, cut four 16-inch-long pieces. These will form the **SEAT**. (Save the leftover board for the next step.)

3 From the remaining ¾-inch-thick board, cut two pieces 9½ inches long. Lay these on your work surface horizontally. From the lower left-hand corner of one piece, measure 1½ inches up the 5½-inch side. From this point, draw a 15° line toward the upper right-hand corner of the piece. See image **b**. From the upper right-hand corner, draw a line down to the lower edge at a 10° angle. Connect the two lines with a horizontal line 2½ inches from the top edge. Do this for the other piece as well and cut out the shapes you've defined. Both pieces should look exactly the same. These will be the **SIDE BOLSTERS** for the **SEAT**. See images **d** and **f**.

4 From the rest of the ¾-inch-thick board, cut a 2-foot-long piece and rip it down to 4 inches wide. This will be the **SPOILER**.

5 From the 14-foot 1-×-5½-inch Ipe wood board, cut four 2-foot-long pieces. These will form the **AXLES**. (You'll use the leftover board in the next step.)

6 From the remaining 1-×-5½-inch board, cut two 16-inch-long pieces. Lay them both down on your work surface so that they're oriented vertically. Starting at the lower-left corner on each board, measure 2 inches up the left-hand side and draw a line at a 10° angle to the top of the board. Cut to the line and keep the larger piece.

Now from the top right-hand corner, use your carpenter's square to draw a line horizontally across the board at a 10° angle. Cut off the small piece at the top. Do the same for the other 16-inch piece. See images **b**, **c**, and **e**. These will be the **SPOILER SUPPORTS**. (Save your leftover board for the next step.)

7 From the remaining 1-inch-thick board, cut off a 7-inch-long piece for the **REAR AXLE BRACE**.

8 Now we're going to cut an even point into what's left of the 1-inch-thick board. There should be a locking position on your chop saw at 31.6°. Set that angle and lock it. Mark the center of one of the short ends of the board and cut to that mark. Turn the board over and do the same thing. Set the chop saw back to 0° and cut the board off 4 inches from the tip of the point. This will be the **STEERING STOPPER**. See **Making the Steering Stopper**.

9 Line up the cut-off, 5½-inch side of the **STEERING STOPPER** on center with the rounded end of the **FRAME**. Now, using the frame as a template, transfer the curve of the **FRAME** to the **STEERING STOPPER** and cut to the line. We have yet to drill the holes, but you should end up with a piece that looks like image **g**.

10 Find one of the **AXLE** pieces that you made in Step 5 and put it horizontally on your work surface. Make a pencil line along the length of the board, 1 inch from the bottom edge. Do the same 1 inch from the top edge. Measuring from one of the short sides of the board, cross both the pencil lines with marks at 1½ inches, 6 inches, 18 inches, and 22½ inches. See **Marking the Holes for the Axles**.

11 Now at all eight of your marks, drill a ½-inch-wide hole ¼ inch into the board. Don't go all the way through—these will be the countersinks for the heads of the carriage bolts. Now change to a ¼-inch bit and drill each hole through the rest of the way. Using this piece as a

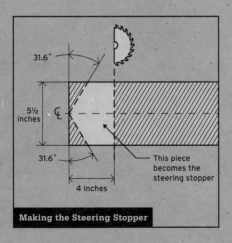

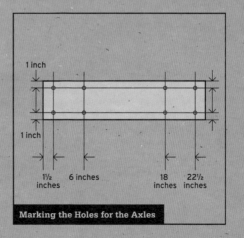

Making the Steering Stopper

31.6°

5½ inches

31.6°

4 inches

This piece becomes the steering stopper

Marking the Holes for the Axles

1 inch

1 inch

1½ inches

6 inches

18 inches

22½ inches

h

j

i

g k

l m

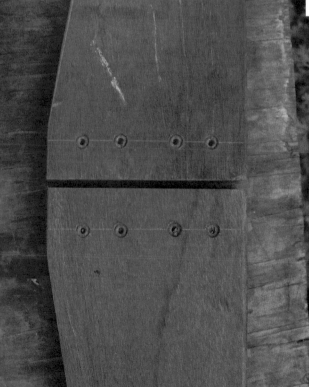

template, drill ¼-inch holes through the rest of the **AXLE** pieces. In one of the three **AXLE** pieces, drill a set of countersinks as you did in the first piece.

12 Now let's assemble the **AXLES**. Each one will be made of a countersunk board on top of a non-countersunk board attached by means of eight 2½-inch carriage bolts. Be sure to put a washer over the threaded end of each carriage bolt before you attach the nuts. Tighten firmly.

13 Let's make one of these **AXLES** the **REAR AXLE** and the other the **FRONT AXLE**. Grab the **REAR AXLE** and, on the same lines you marked earlier, make marks at 10 inches and 14 inches from the short edge. You should have two marks on each line.

14 Drill a ¼-inch hole all the way through the **REAR AXLE** at each mark.

15 Drill a ½-inch hole through the centerline of the **FRAME**, 8 inches back from the rounded end.

16 Grab the **FRONT AXLE** and make a mark at a point 2¾ inches from the long edge and 12 inches from either short end. This should be the exact center of the axle. Drill a ½-inch hole all the way through this point.

17 Place the ½-×-4½-inch carriage bolt down through the ½-inch hole in the **FRAME** and the ½-inch hole in **FRONT AXLE**. Now add a washer and a nut. Tighten the nut down very tightly and then loosen it until you can smoothly move the **FRONT AXLE** back and forth. Put a crescent wrench or a ¾-inch box wrench on the nut and screw another nut down on top of it. Tighten the second one very tightly while holding the first one steady. See images **h** and **j**.

18 Let's attach the **STEERING STOPPER** now. Line it up, round end to round end, on the centerline of the **FRAME**. To determine where to place the **STOPPER**, slide it closer to the **FRONT AXLE**. Ensure that the **AXLE**, when it swings, butts up perfectly against the **STOPPER**. See **Positioning the Steering Stopper**. Once you've found the correct spot, mark the **STOPPER**'s position on the **FRAME**. To attach it, drill three ¼-inch holes in a triangular pattern on the **STOPPER**, making sure to drill them in at least 1 inch from any edge. Once you've drilled the holes, reposition the **STOPPER** on the **FRAME** and drill a

matching set of holes using the **STOPPER** as a template. Countersink the holes on the top side of **FRAME** using a ½-inch spade bit. Attach using 2½-inch carriage bolts, nuts, and washers. See image **i**.

19 Now let's move on to the other end of the **FRAME**. On the bottom side of the frame, draw a line horizontally across the **FRAME** 8 inches from the back end, and another line 13½ inches from the back end.

20 Place the **REAR AXLE** exactly between these lines, making sure it's centered on the **FRAME**. Clamp it down and drill through the existing holes in the **AXLE**, extending them all the way through the **FRAME**. On the top side of the **FRAME**, countersink the four holes with the ½-inch spade bit. Now attach the **AXLE** to the **FRAME** using the four 3½-inch carriage bolts, nuts, and washers. Make sure that they're very tight and that the heads of the bolts don't protrude above the surface of the **FRAME**. Alright! Both **AXLES** are now on! See image **i**.

21 Find the **REAR AXLE BRACE** from Step 7 and draw a line exactly down the middle of it lengthwise. Drill a ½-inch hole 1 inch from each edge, on the centerline. Place the **BRACE** on the **FRAME** directly in line with the **REAR AXLE**. Clamp the **BRACE** onto the **FRAME** and transfer the holes, but don't go all the way through. Now pull the **BRACE** off and continue drilling the holes 2½ inches into the **FRAME** and the **AXLE**. Again, don't go all the way through.

22 Put the **REAR AXLE BRACE** back in place. Then put a washer on each of the two ⅜-×-3-inch lag bolts and drive one into each hole, securing them tightly. See image **k**.

23 Find the **SPOILER SUPPORTS** from Step 6. Draw a line 1 inch up from, and parallel to, the 5½-inch (bottom) edge. The side with the long 10° cut out of it is the front edge. From this front edge, drill ¹¹⁄₆₄-inch holes at 1 inch, 2 inches, 3½ inches, and 4½ inches along the 1-inch line you just drew. Countersink each of the holes with a ⅜-inch bit to ⅛ inch deep. Do the same thing to the other **SPOILER SUPPORT**. When you countersink the holes, keep in mind that you need to make left- and right-side **SUPPORTS**. Make sure the countersinks will face outwards on both sides of the cart. See image **l**.

n

o

p

q

24 Line up the **SPOILER SUPPORTS** with the **REAR AXLE** and **REAR AXLE BRACE**. Using the **SUPPORTS** as a template, transfer the four holes to the **BRACE** and **FRAME** with the $^{11}/_{64}$-inch bit. The holes will go exactly between the two pieces—that's okay. You should still predrill. Ipe is hard to work with if you don't.

25 Attach the two **SPOILER SUPPORTS** using eight 12-×-2-inch stainless steel screws. Put the drill on the "Slow/Torque" setting and really press into the screws as you drive them in. Don't strip the heads, or they'll be really hard to get out. See image **n**.

26 Grab the **SPOILER** from Step 4. Looking down at the top of it, we want to round off the two corners on the front edge to a radius of 2¾ inches or so. (The front edge is the long edge that you didn't cut.) Now let's attach it to the tops of the **SPOILER SUPPORTS**, keeping the front edges of both pieces flush with each other. When lined up with the centerline of the cart, the outer edge of the **SPOILER** will be 7½ inches from the outside edge of either **SUPPORT** and cantilever off the back edge by about ½ inch. Now make two lines from front to back on the **SPOILER**, each 8 inches from the outer edges. On each of these lines make marks at 1 inch and 2 inches from the front edge. With the $^{11}/_{64}$-inch bit, drill holes through the **SPOILER** at these marks, then drill down ⅛ inch with the ⅜-inch bit to countersink.

27 Line up the **SPOILER** centered on the **SUPPORTS** and, using it as a template, transfer the holes 2 inches into the **SUPPORTS** with the $^{11}/_{64}$-inch bit. You may need a hand to hold the **SPOILER** steady as you drill. Attach using four 12-×-2-inch stainless steel screws. Again, set the drill to "Slow/Torque" and really press to get the screws to sink in. They should be flush so that the kids don't feel them when they hang on. See image **r**.

28 Now find the four **SEAT** pieces from Step 2. On one of the pieces, round off two of the corners along one of the longer edges. See **Rounding of the Go-Cart Seat Corners**. Do this to one other piece as well. These two pieces will form the front and top of the **SEAT**. See **Go-Cart Exploded View**.

29 Pick one of the round-cornered pieces and one of the straight seat pieces to be the bottom section of the **SEAT**. Draw centerlines across these pieces in both directions (longitudinally and laterally). Make marks on each of the lateral centerlines 5½ inches from each end, so that you have two marks on each of the bottom **SEAT** pieces. Now we'll place the **SEAT** in place on the **FRAME**. Place a scrap piece of ¾-inch-thick wood against the **SPOILER SUPPORTS** as a spacer. Add a regular **SEAT** piece, then another ¾-inch spacer, then one of the rounded **SEAT** pieces. Line up the longitudinal center lines of the **SEAT** pieces and the **FRAME**. Press everything snugly together (see image **m**) and clamp the bottom **SEAT** pieces in place.

30 At each of the 5½-inch marks, drill ¼ inch down with a ½-inch bit to countersink, then follow up with a ¼-inch bit and drill through both the **SEAT** and the **FRAME**. Place a 2½-inch carriage bolt into each hole and secure the **SEAT** bottoms to the **FRAME** with washers and nuts.

31 Now let's attach the backrest. Lay the ¾-inch spacer on the **SEAT** bottom, which you just attached. Lay the remaining straight **SEAT** piece against the **SPOILER SUPPORTS**, add another ¾-inch spacer on top of this, and then add the second rounded **SEAT** piece. Make sure the **SEAT** pieces are on center—their outer edges should be 3½ inches from the outer edges of the **SPOILER SUPPORTS**. When you have them aligned, transfer the imaginary centerlines of the front edges of the **SPOILER SUPPORTS** to the front face of each **SEAT** piece. See image **t**.

32 From the top edge of each **SEAT** piece, measure down 1½ inches and 4 inches along the lines you just drew and mark those points. Set the **UPPER SEAT** piece aside for now. At all four marks on the **LOWER** (straight) **SEAT** piece, drill a ⅜-inch hole for countersinking (⅛ inch deep) and then follow up by drilling 2 inches deep with the ¹¹⁄₆₄-inch bit through the **SEAT** pieces and into the **SPOILER SUPPPORTS**.

33 Bury the 12-×-2-inch stainless steel screws into the holes of the lower rung of the **SEAT**, using the same technique as before (in Steps 25 and 27).

34 Repeat the previous two steps for the upper **SEAT** piece, ensuring that you use a ¾-inch spacer to position it correctly. Don't forget that the rounded corners should be facing up.

35 Okay, we're into the home stretch now. Find the **SIDE BOLSTERS** from Step 3. They should fit lengthwise on top of the bottom half of the **SEAT**, flush with its outer edges, and butt up against the back edge of the **SEAT**. See image **u**. Attach each **BOLSTER** using four stainless steel screws: three through the bottom of the **SEAT** and one through the backrest into the **BOLSTER**. Before attaching, predrill and countersink the holes using the ¹¹⁄₆₄-inch bit and ⅜-inch bit respectively. See image **s** and **u**. Be careful not to drill all the way through the **BOLSTER**—including the depth of the bottom **SEAT**, you can drill 2 inches deep. See image **r**.

36 So that we can steer this slick little machine, let's install a steering line. To start, drill a ¾-inch-wide hole, at about a 30° angle, down through both sides of the **FRONT AXLE** at points 2 inches from the back edge and 1½ inches from the outside edges. From the top of the **AXLE**, drill toward the front of the cart. See image **p**.

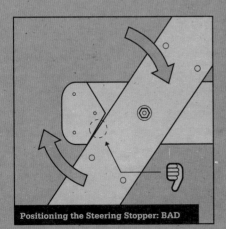

Positioning the Steering Stopper: BAD

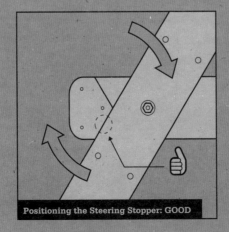

Positioning the Steering Stopper: GOOD

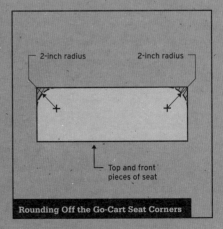

Rounding Off the Go-Cart Seat Corners

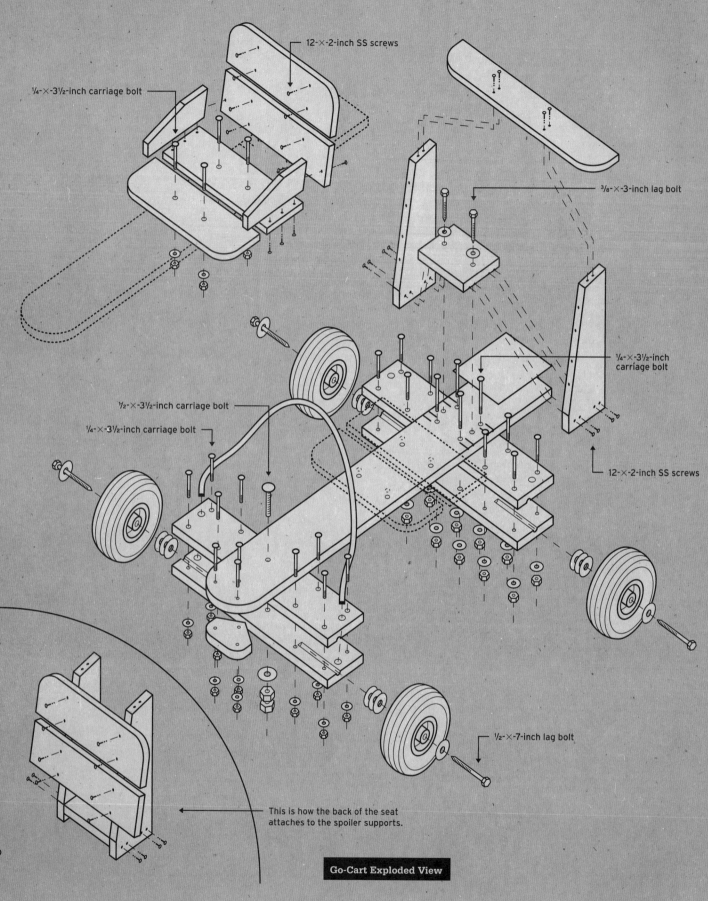

12-×-2-inch SS screws

¼-×-3½-inch carriage bolt

⅜-×-3-inch lag bolt

¼-×-3½-inch carriage bolt

12-×-2-inch SS screws

½-×-3½-inch carriage bolt

¼-×-3½-inch carriage bolt

½-×-7-inch lag bolt

This is how the back of the seat attaches to the spoiler supports.

Go-Cart Exploded View

37 Now here come the wheels! Let's mount the front wheels slightly forward of the **AXLE** centerline so that we don't get high-speed, foot-to-wheel contact. Make a mark 2½ inches from the front edge of the **AXLE** piece, right where the two boards of the **AXLE** meet. At this mark, drill straight in with the ⅜-inch spade bit to a depth of 6 inches. Check the angle frequently to ensure you're drilling straight between the two boards. Do the same thing on the other side.

38 Place a 1½-inch washer over a 7½-inch lag bolt and fit it through the wheel, making sure that the wheel is facing the right way. (There's usually a long plastic piece on the inside of the wheel to keep it from rubbing against the **AXLE**.) Now place three additional washers on the lag bolt (on the other side of the wheel) and drive it into the 6-inch hole using a ¾-inch socket wrench. Make it tight, then back off a bit until the wheel spins freely. Do the same thing on the other side. Lube the wheel and bolt if you find that they stick. Again, I recommend 8-inch wheels with metal hubs and bearings. The ride will be smoother and quicker. See images **q** and **o**.

39 Now drill ⅜-×-6-inch holes into the center of each side of the **REAR AXLE**. To find the center, measure

2¾ inches from the **AXLE**'s front edge, along the seam line. Attach the wheels as in the previous step.

40 Now grab the rope, heat and duct-tape the ends to keep it from fraying, and then feed one end through the holes in the **AXLE** that you drilled in Step 36. Tie a stopper knot in both ends leaving only 1 inch of slack, so the rope doesn't drag when you're speeding downhill. Tie them tight!

41 You're almost done! First it's sanding time, though. Using your electric sander and 60-grit paper, sand all the wooden surfaces. Hold the sander at a 45° angle to take off all the sharp edges. If you sand it enough, you'll go through about five sheets of sandpaper.

42 Clean off the dust and stick the grip tape to the platform formed by the **FRAME** at the back of the cart.

43 Now hand your young racer some driving gloves so he (or she!) and a friend can head for the hills, literally. One can steer while the other hangs off the back. A few skateboard-style kicks are all it takes to get things rolling! Driver and kicker can switch after every run. Formula training starts here!

KNOTS

First a few words about rope. With any piece of rope, we can refer to three different parts: the end, the standing part, and the bight. The end is, well, the very end of the rope. The standing part is the part of the rope that's attached to an object, or if the rope isn't attached to anything, it's the unused part toward the middle of the rope. The bight is a U-shaped loop between the end and the standing part of the rope.

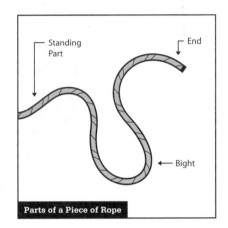

Parts of a Piece of Rope

A **STOPPER KNOT** (sometimes called a figure-8 knot) works well to keep the end of a rope from going through a hole. To form a stopper knot, make a bight in the rope and cross the end of it over and under the standing part (**Step 1**). Now pass the end of the rope through the bight, making sure to bring it down from the top, not up from underneath (**Step 2**). Pull it tight, and you should end up with a knot that looks like a figure 8 (**Step 3**).

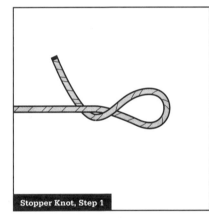

Stopper Knot, Step 1

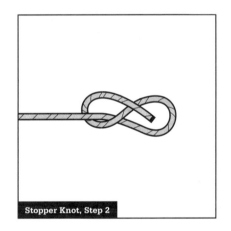

Stopper Knot, Step 2

A **SHEET BEND** is especially handy for tying two pieces of rope together that are of different diameters. To start, make a bight in the thicker piece of line. Pass the end of your thinner rope through the bight, then around the outside of it. To finish it off, pass the end of the thinner rope between its own standing part and the bight of the thicker rope without going back through the loop of the

Stopper Knot, Step 3

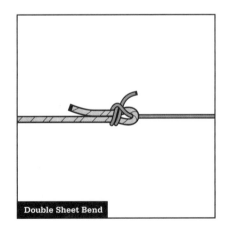

Double Sheet Bend

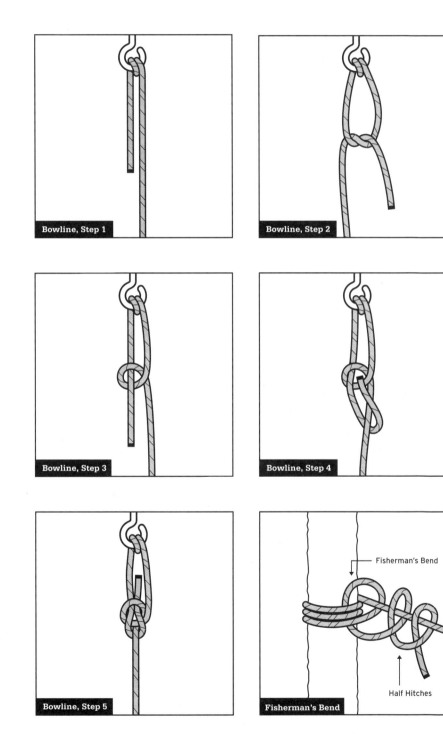

Bowline, Step 1

Bowline, Step 2

Bowline, Step 3

Bowline, Step 4

Bowline, Step 5

Fisherman's Bend

Half Hitches

Fisherman's Bend

bight. I know this sounds confusing, but one look at the illustration will clear things up. To make it extra secure, take the thinner rope two turns around the bight of the thicker rope before finishing off the knot. That's called a double sheet bend.

A **BOWLINE** is a solid knot that locks against itself to form a non-slipping loop, so it's very secure. If you take an extra turn around the object you're tying to, it will help prevent rope chafe. Let's say we'll be tying to an eyebolt. Take a turn around the eye with the rope. This means passing the end through the eye, pulling it down and passing it through the eye again in the same direction **(Step 1)**. Now tie a simple overhand knot **(Step 2)** and pull the end tight to form a threaded loop in the standing part **(Step 3)**. Now pass the end behind the standing part and back through the loop **(Steps 4–5)**. Now you've a got good, solid, low-wear knot for all your swinging and climbing needs.

A **FISHERMAN'S BEND** is another super-solid knot. We'll use it to tie around a tree in the Rope Bridge project. To make this knot, wrap the rope around the tree three times. Then pass the end around the standing part of the rope and back through the three loops. Make sure the wraps are tight, and finish the knot off with a couple of half hitches.

To make a half hitch, pass the end of the rope around the standing part and then back through the loop that you've just formed. Make another half hitch and you're done.

A **SQUARE KNOT** (called a *reef knot* in the sailing world) is usually used as a temporary knot to join two pieces of identical line. We'll be taping it down in the Water-Balloon Launcher project, so no worries there. This is a very simple knot to tie. It starts with a simple overhand knot, just like the first part of tying your shoes **(Step 1)**. (The knot we use to tie our shoes is actually a double-slipped square knot.) To finish the knot tie another overhand knot on top of the one you just made. The only trick here is to make sure that each piece of rope enters and exits the knot on the same side **(Step 2)**. If you get this wrong you'll end up with a granny knot, which isn't very stable and is hard to untie if it's tight. See **Granny Knot**. If you need to untie a tight square knot, just grab the standing part and the end of one of the pieces of rope in the knot and pull them apart. This will break the knot.

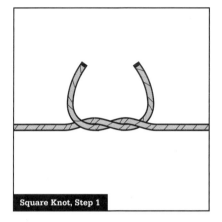

Square Knot, Step 1

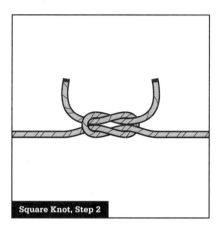

Square Knot, Step 2

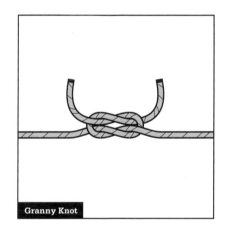

Granny Knot

RESOURCES

ART SUPPLIES

www.flaxart.com

www.misterart.com

www.pearlpaint.com

www.lonestarcandlesupply.com

BIRD FEED

www.coleswildbird.com

www.audubonworkshop.com

CLIMBING SUPPLIES

www.indoorclimbing.com

www.atomikclimbingholds.com

FABRIC SUPPLIES

www.fabricandart.com

www.discountfabricsusacorp.com

www.discountfabrics-sf.com

LIGHTS

www.ikea.com

LUMBER

www.sierrapointlumber.com

www.stockbuildingsupply.com

www.advantagelumber.com

PLEXIGLAS

www.eplastics.com

ROPE

www.us-rope-cable.com

www.e-rigging.com

www.contractorsrope.com

www.lehighgroup.com

SKATEBOARD SUPPLIES

www.warehouseskateboards.com

www.skateboards.com

STEEL CABLE

www.gbgindustries.com

www.outdoorfunstore.com

www.ropescourse.us

SURGICAL TUBING

www.reefscuba.com

TURKEY FEATHERS

www.ostrich.com

INDEX